THE
NEW AGE
COUNTERFEIT

A STUDY GUIDE FOR INDIVIDUAL OR GROUP USE

By:
Johnnette S. Benkovic

Published by:

Queenship
P.O. Box 220
Goleta, CA 93116

Originally published and distributed by:
Living His Life Abundantly®
702 Bayview Ave.
Clearwater, Florida 34619

Copyright © 1993: Johnette S. Benkovic

Library of Congress Catalog Card No.: 95-074824

ISBN: 1-57918-138-4

Nihil obstat: The Reverend Harold Bumpus
Censor Librorum

Imprimatur: Most Reverend John C. Favalora
Bishop of St. Petersburg
March 4, 1993

Published by:
Queenship Publishing
PO Box 220
Goleta, CA 93116
(800) 647-9882 / (805) 692-0043
Fax (805) 967-5843

Printed in United States of America

Cover design by: Peg Heimlich
Vorhis Art
Terrace Park, Ohio 45174

Contents

Acknowledgments

Many people deserve credit for this study guide. I thank my staff at *LIVING HIS LIFE ABUNDANTLY*®· my lay association of the *Marian Servants of Divine Providence*, the *Franciscan University of Steubenville*, and Bill Reck and Jayne Dillon of *The Riehle Foundation*.

But most of all, I thank my family, especially my husband, Anthony. My Anthony has been a constant companion, listener, and advisor throughout the writing of this study guide. He has lifted my spirits when they were down, helped me to keep my ultimate goal in focus, and reminded me to keep my eyes on Jesus every step of the way.

Finally, I thank Our Lord Jesus Christ who loves each one of us unconditionally, even a sinner like me. I thank our Blessed Mother whose intercession for this project I beseeched each day. And I thank the Holy Spirit for the graces of perseverance and faith.

Preface

We are called to be sons and daughters of God but we are not gods. All that we are and have come from God.

The fundamental error of the New Age Movement distorts this beautiful reality of God's plan for us. It asserts that we can become God by becoming aware of and developing the human potential within us. Tragically, this movement is drawing large numbers of people into this erroneous and harmful way of life and it is having strong influence in so many areas of human life and society.

Mrs. Johnnette Benkovic provides a much needed service for Christians in this study guide, *The New Age Counterfeit,* explaining the ideas and sources of the New Age Movement, its large influence in society, and the various ways in which it distorts Christian thinking. She exposes the false principle that humanity saves itself as well as the many ways this is expressed, and clearly states the Gospel proclamation that salvation is only found in Jesus Christ.

The study questions and Scripture passages found at the end of each chapter are quite useful. They are aids to prayer and reflection on what we have read in the chapter, to personal examination of conscience, and to group study. And with Scripture we root ourselves in God's inspired Word as we deal with these issues. The entire study guide assists in assimilating the solid material produced in recent years studying the New Age Movement.

Jesus Christ is the Savior of the entire human race. Only in Him are we reconciled to God. He, the Son of God, is the Way, the Truth, and the Life. He is the one and only path to God. He is the Revelation of God. He is God's Son and the one and only source of God's Life coming into us. He tells us not to have itching ears listening to false doctrines. He is the Kingdom of God present among us. In Him and through His Church we have life, abundant life.

We can be grateful to Johnnette Benkovic for proclaiming so clearly the basic Gospel truths concerning salvation in Christ, and pointing out with equal clarity the errors and false hopes for salvation contained in the New Age Movement, a movement which is indeed a counterfeit of the true reality.

> Father Daniel Sinisi, T.O.R.
> Associate Professor of Theology
> Franciscan University of Steubenville

"Am I not here who am your mother?"

This study guide is dedicated to Our Lady of Guadalupe. As she crushed the head of the stone serpent in 1531, may she crush the head of the serpent in our midst today, and lead us to her Son, Our Lord Jesus Christ, Who is the Way, the Truth, and the Life!

Prayer to the Holy Spirit

Come, O Holy Spirit
Fill the hearts of Your faithful,
and kindle in them the fire of Your love.
Send forth Your Spirit,
and they shall be created,
and You shall renew the face of the earth.

O God, Who did instruct the hearts of the faithful
by the light of the Holy Spirit,
grant us in the same Spirit to be truly wise
and ever to rejoice in His consolation,
through Jesus Christ Our Lord,

Amen

How To Use This Study Guide

The following Scripture Study Guide has been developed to complement the television series, **THE NEW AGE: SATAN'S COUNTERFEIT,** produced by *Living His Life Abundantly®* and *Franciscan University of Steubenville.* As such, it provides a concise overview of each aspect of the New Age Movement considered in the television series. For a more in-depth analysis of any of these aspects, a complete bibliography has been provided.

The study guide can be used independently of the television series, however, and is especially conducive for parish study groups and adult education classes. It can also be used effectively by individuals.

The objectives for this study guide are 1) to help the individual come to a deeper understanding of the New Age Movement and its philosophical underpinnings; 2) to illustrate the incompatibility of New Age thinking with Christian truth; 3) to call attention to some of the ways New Age ideas have infiltrated Christian circles; and 4) to anchor the individual into an authentic spirituality based on the revealed truth of Sacred Scripture and the teachings of the Roman Catholic Church.

As mentioned, we have prepared the study guide to be used individually or in a small group setting. If it is used in a group, the number of people per group should exceed no more than nine individuals plus one facilitator so that each member will have an opportunity to express his or her thoughts and ideas about the *Questions for Reflection* and *Scripture Passages for Meditation.* In a group setting, the thoughts and reflections about the Scripture passages from the preceding week should be shared prior to the new week's topic.

We also recommend that each person using this study guide keep a journal throughout the course of the study. All participants should record their thoughts, ideas, insights, and inspirations as they ponder the *Questions for Reflection* and *Scripture Passages for Meditation*. This will provide participants with a marvelous testimony of God's interaction with them and the movement of the Holy Spirit in their own lives.

Finally, the Scripture passages given are meant to form the basis of a prayer time throughout the course of each week. All of the passages selected are related to the topic under consideration. We strongly suggest using the *lectio-divina* method of praying Scripture. For those who are new to this method, the following acronym P-R-A-Y provides an easy and effective way to formulate this time of prayer:

First, *PRAY* for the guidance of the Holy Spirit during this time of prayer, and open your mind and heart to receive all that Our Lord has to give you.

Then prayerfully and thoughtfully *READ* the Scripture passage.

Next, *ASK* and ponder these three questions:
1. What does this passage mean contextually and in the culture of the time?
2. What is God saying to me through this passage?
3. What is my response to God about what He has revealed to me through this passage?

Finally, *YIELD* to the presence of God, sit quietly with Him, and let His word take root in your heart.

As you receive this study guide, know that our prayers are with you. Please remember us in yours.

WEEK ONE

"For the time will come when people will not tolerate sound doctrine, but, following their own desires, will surround themselves with teachers who tickle their ears. They will stop listening to the truth and will wander off to fables. As for you, be steady and self-possessed; put up with hardship, perform your work as an evangelist, fulfill your ministry."
—2 Timothy 4: 3-5

An Overview of the New Age Movement

A leaderless but powerful network is working to bring about radical change in the United States. Its members have broken with certain key elements of Western thought, and they may even have broken continuity with history . . . This network is the Aquarian Conspiracy . . . Broader than reform, deeper than revolution, this benign conspiracy for a new human agenda has triggered the most rapid cultural realignment in history . . . It is a new mind—the ascendance of a startling worldview that gathers into its framework breakthrough science and insights from earliest recorded thought . . . The crises of our time . . . are the necessary impetus for the revolution now underway . . . We are living in the change of change, the time in which we can intentionally align ourselves with nature for rapid remaking of ourselves and our collapsing institutions. The paradigm of the Aquarian Conspiracy sees humankind embedded in nature . . . Human nature is neither good nor bad but open to continuous transformation and transcendence . . . It has only to discover itself.[1]

This excerpt is from Marilyn Ferguson's book, *The Aquarian Conspiracy: Personal and Social Transformation in Our Time.* Her writings have helped to establish the New Age Movement. Here is a brief description of the motive, method, and goal of the

---

1. Marilyn Ferguson, *The Aquarian Conspiracy: Personal and Social Transformation in Our Times* (Los Angeles, California: Jeremy Tarcher, 1980), p. 23.

1

New Age Movement. The motive: a resolution must be found for the crises of our time. The method: a discovery of the transformative and transcendent powers latent in human nature. The goal: a "new human" agenda capable of ushering in an age of peace, harmony, and unity.[2]

As stated in the excerpt from *The Aquarian Conspiracy,* the New Age Movement believes that human nature is *inherently* capable of continuous transformation and transcendence. A person's real problem is ignorance of his or her true potential, a problem supposedly created by Western civilization which has taught that man has limitations and finitude. The solution, according to New Age proponents, is to break through to a new consciousness that at once shows man his limitless potential and his ultimate reality—his own divinity. As more and more individuals become "enlightened" to this reality, New Agers believe that a critical shift in consciousness throughout the species will take place, and all mankind will come to "god consciousness." Thus, the ultimate step in the evolutionary process will have been completed.

The first step, then, is for vast numbers of individuals to become "enlightened" and personally transformed. The enlightenment that the New Ager strives to attain is a new worldview, a new perspective of seeing reality. The foundational element in this new perspective is monism, a philosophy teaching that everything is "interrelated, interdependent, and interpenetrating."[3] God is not a personal God, but rather an impersonal energy force that permeates all things. Therefore, God, man, the dolphin, and the rain forest are all part of a continuous reality. Any apparent differences are not real and are only illusions. Fritjof Capra, physicist and philosopher, writes in his book, *Turning Point,* that the ultimate state of consciousness is one "in which all boundaries and dualisms have been transcended and all individuality dissolves into universal, undifferentiated oneness."[4] For the New Ager, this "oneness" obliterates even the distinction between

---

2. Quotes my own.
3. Douglas Groothuis, *Unmasking the New Age* (Downers Grove, Illinois: Intervarsity Press, 1986), p. 18.
4. Groothuis, *Unmasking the New Age,* p. 19. Quote from Fritjof Capra, *The Turning Point* (New York: Simon and Schuster, 1982), p. 371.

good and evil, which is "dualism." Decisions are based on situational ethics instead of moral absolutes.

This monistic worldview is gained through any number of consciousness-altering techniques which are called entry points. Says Ferguson, "All of these approaches might be called psychotechnologies—systems for a deliberate change in consciousness."[5] In *The Aquarian Conspiracy*, she lists many entry points: sensory isolation and sensory overload; biofeedback; music; self-help networks; hypnosis and self-hypnosis; meditation; Sufi stories and koans[6]; seminars like est, Silva Mind Control, Lifespring, etc.; dream journals; A Course in Miracles; and many more.[7]

In Our Midst

Douglas Groothuis writes in his book, *Unmasking the New Age,* "But if the transformation is to be complete, it must permeate and overtake the Western mindset. This means nothing less than the infiltration and revision of major intellectual disciplines as well as the common world view of the person on the street. The One must move from the avant-garde fringe to the very heart and mind of society. And this is exactly what is happening."[8] According to her own research and surveys Ferguson states, "The Aquarian Conspirators range across all levels of income and education . . . There are school teachers and office workers, famous scientists, government officials, artists and millionaires, taxi drivers and celebrities, leaders in medicine, education, law, psychology . . . There are legions of conspirators. They are in corporations, universities and hospitals, on the faculties of public schools, in factories and doctors' offices, in state and federal agencies, on city councils and the White House staff, in state legislatures, in volunteer organizations, in virtually all arenas of policy making in the country."[9] Indeed, from art to entertainment, from editorial pages to Sunday sermons, from university class-

---

5. Ferguson, *The Aquarian Conspiracy,* p. 87.
6. For a definition of "koan," see p. 15.
7. Ferguson, *The Aquarian Conspiracy,* pp. 86-87.
8. Groothuis, *Unmasking the New Age,* p. 51.
9. Ferguson, *The Aquarian Conspiracy,* pp. 23-24

rooms to kindergartens, the influence of the New Age Movement is moving contemporary man away from the Judeo-Christian perspective of the world to a monistic idealism.

As Christians, we do not argue against the need to resolve the crises of our time, nor do we look askance at the worthwhile desire to create a world of peace. However, because of its underlying philosophy, we must look critically at the method of approach suggested by Marilyn Ferguson and other proponents of the New Age. This philosophy is in sharp opposition to Christianity. First and foremost, Christianity is monotheistic, not monistic. It teaches that God and His creation are separate and distinct. Secondly, while we admit that transformation is necessary ("Do not conform yourself to this age but be transformed by the renewal of your mind. . . ." *Romans* 12:2), as Christians we know that true transformation comes only through grace and an abiding relationship with Jesus Christ.

Third, mankind's salvation and true peace comes as a result of doing the will of God and living according to His laws. Man's problem is not ignorance of his divinity, but his sin against God. If each person surrenders himself to God's will, and if he lives out that will in his own life, then peace and unity can be attained throughout the world. Finally, the belief that man is God is not new and not true. It was first suggested by the serpent in the Garden of Eden to Adam and Eve (*Genesis* 3:5). Their gullibility led to the first sin and should serve as a warning to all others who would be so easily enticed by the Evil One. While man is not God, he is called into relationship with God through the saving act of Jesus Christ. In Him rests our hope.

In conclusion, St. Paul tells us in *2 Timothy* 4: 3-5 "that there will come a time when people will not tolerate sound doctrine . . . but will surround themselves with teachers who tickle their ears . . . (People) will stop listening to the truth and will wander off to fables." The rapid progress and infiltration of the New Age Movement into all sectors of society seems to indicate the fulfillment of this prophecy. As Christians, we must equip ourselves to recognize the "fable" in our midst and to preach the truth of Jesus Christ when given the opportunity.

Insights Based on First-Hand Experience
An Interview with Chris Noble

For ten years of his life, Chris Noble sought for Truth through the various aspects of the New Age Movement. Ultimately, his quest led him to the faith of his youth, Christianity. He is currently Director of Education for the Diocese of Tulsa and holds a masters degree in Christian Ministry and Renewal. Chris is a doctoral candidate at Duquesne Universtity in Pittsburgh, Pennsylvania.

Johnnette: As we begin to consider the New Age Movement, I think it is important for us to start off with a definition. What is the New Age Movement and what are its goals?

Chris: It is a movement that is sociological and religious, and from a Catholic point of view it is a movement of false spirituality. It really is a movement that is out to change significantly the way America and the world thinks. At the core of the New Age Movement, I found an anti-Christian set of ideas and presuppositions. The New Age is a synthesis of Eastern mysticism, Eastern religions, and Western Occultism. These two streams have been packaged in psychological scientific jargon. Also the New Age is a syncretistic type of movement. What that means is that it takes from anywhere, any body of knowledge of any kind of organization, and mixes things all up together. So many of the New Age organizations have a whole variety of teachings which usually come under a very strong and very charismatic leader. Another hallmark of the New Age is they believe in, well, you've heard of the Age of Aquarius, it's the coming New Age. It's kind of a utopian vision of one world unity, harmony, and peace that is accomplished through a one-world government and a one-world religion. This is a goal of many of the New Age organizations.

Johnnette: When you think about those goals—peace and unity in the world—they sound like pretty healthy goals. What's the matter with the New Age approach to these goals, Chris?

Chris: Well, everybody wants peace, harmony, and unity, that's true. But the question is how do you take all of the variety of peoples and cultures in the world and bring them under one government. That sounds like a tyrannical type of approach or government to me. And also, only God can accomplish this type of unity and harmony. The real government of the world is the Kingdom of God on earth, and when men try to take the governments of the world and try to bring them under one set of ideas, one religion, one government, they are trying to take the place of God. And I think that's basically what is wrong with this idea of one-world government.

Johnnette: In speaking about God, there is a term that we often hear through New Agers and in New Age literature, and it is "christ-consciousness." Who is Jesus Christ to the New Age Movement?

Chris: For the New Age Movement, Jesus Christ is not the Incarnation of the Second Person of the Blessed Trinity, God-man, our Savior, and our Lord. That's not what the [term] means. "Christ-consciousness" means we can all become conscious, we all can become enlightened like Christ. Christ was simply one example. He was one of many gurus, he was one of many teachers, and we can all become like Christ and surpass Him. We can all have this cosmic consciousness, this one consciousness, this unified consciousness of the whole world like Christ. And He's not special or different or unique. He's just one who came before us.

Johnnette: This is very different from Catholic teaching where Jesus is the Second Person of the Blessed Trinity. You talked about the fact that there are many different streams and the syncretistic approach of the New Age Movement. Are there some common underlying premises of the New Age Movement?

Chris: Yes. When I was in the New Age I began to see common underlying themes that were present in every organization I was in. I think the most common theme I found is that they say we are all gods. We are all divine. We're either going to become a god, or we are one right now. That was the main theme I found. As you know, this is totally opposed to any kind of Christian teaching. Another theme I found is called pantheism which is an ancient teaching and all it means is that all is god. The sun is god, the mountains are god, the trees are god, the animals are god, and we are god. And we're not any different from anything else. We're all god. Another teaching that goes along with pantheism, also ancient, nothing new, is called monism. Very similar to pantheism, it means all is one. And the basic premise of this teaching is that we're not different. There's only one personality in the whole universe. There's not you or I as distinct people. There's not millions of different entities. There's just one thing and that one thing is God. All else is illusion. Another theme I find throughout the New Age is called "transformation of consciousness." It's a lot like christ-consciousness that we've talked about. Through meditation or some kind of technique, I lose my identity as an individual and I become one with this world consciousness, like a wave in an ocean or a drop in the sea. We have a transformed consciousness and that's what all life is about, this enlightened consciousness. To go with that is this notion of unlimited human potential. The Human Potential Movement kind of evolved into this. And the basic idea behind this is that we all have these psychic powers—out of body experiences, ESP, clairvoyant experiences—we all have these psychic powers and we develop these along the lines of a spiritual evolution.

Johnnette: Chris, when you're speaking about all of these things they sound very foreign. But these ideas are beginning to bombard us in our society and culture. How are we seeing these ideas being manifested?

Chris: We see them everywhere. At business seminars. It's in education. It's in the health fields. It's permeating our culture in all kinds of ways and I think the biggest danger is that these new ideas are being absorbed with techniques and practices that are virtually untested. And they're simply assumed to be true. They haven't been tested by any of the professionals in those fields.

Johnnette: You talk about these things as if there is a danger attached. What draws people into the New Age Movement and what are the dangers?

Chris: I think people get drawn in for many different reasons. I got drawn in because at a young age—fourteen or fifteen—I rejected Christianity. I wanted to strike out on my own, but I still wanted some meaning in my life. My life was becoming empty and I couldn't find a real foothold on what my life was all about. And so I began to search in the New Age to find out what I was doing, why I was here, and what was the meaning of life. But I also think people begin to dabble. It looks very interesting. It looks fascinating—Ouija boards, tarot cards—they look very fun. But you get hooked, you get drawn it. I also think people are involved in it because they want to control other people's lives. And they have. Personally, I think they have evil intents.

Questions for Reflection

1. What are the goals of the New Age Movement? What type of people are likely to be involved with this movement?
2. How is the New Age Movement in opposition to Christianity?
3. What examples of the New Age Movement do I encounter in my everyday life? What can I do to resist and combat these influences?
4. Who is Jesus Christ to me and to what extent am I surrendered to His Lordship and will?
5. Considering my personality, weaknesses and strengths, what aspects of my personhood could lead me in the direction of the New Age Movement?

Scripture Passages for Meditation

Day One: *2 Timothy* 4: 3-5
Day Two: *Ezekiel* 3: 1-11
Day Three: *2 Corinthians* 5: 17-21
Day Four: *2 Corinthians* 11: 13-15
Day Five: *Galatians* 5: 19-25
Day Six: *1 John* 1: 6-10
Day Seven: *1 Peter* 3: 15-17

> *"You have not drawn near to an untouchable mountain and a
> blazing fire, nor gloomy darkness and storm . . . No, you have
> drawn near to Mount Zion and the city of the living God . . . to
> Jesus, the mediator of a new covenant . . . ."*
> —Hebrews 12: 18, 22, 24

Eastern Oriental Philosophy:
Hinduism and Buddhism

The New Age Movement is syncretistic. That is, it is a mixture of many different ideologies. While it takes bits and pieces from various belief systems, it remains totally faithful to none, and changes concepts, tenets and ideas to suit its own purposes. One strain from which it has drawn heavily is the belief system of Eastern religions, specifically Hinduism and Buddhism.

Hinduism

The worldview of Hinduism is very different from that of Christianity. Hinduism is polytheistic, pantheistic, and monistic.[1] Hinduism teaches that everything in the universe, animate or inanimate, has the same divine nature called Brahman (god).[2] Brahman is the only reality. All else is illusion (maya) and does not really exist. "For Hinduism, the body and mind, like other material objects, are merely illusory appearances. When this is realized, the only reality that remains is *atman* or self. The self is none other than Brahman or god . . . The *true self* is god. The *I* which I consider myself to be is in reality the *not-self*. This not-self is caught in a world of illusion, ignorance, and bondage . . . You must lose your personal ego-consciousness into god. You

---

1. **Polytheism**—the belief and worship of many gods. **Pantheism**—a belief that all things are essentially God. **Monism**—the doctrine that reality is an indivisible, universal force.
2. Walter Martin, *The New Cults* (Santa Ana, California: Vision House, 1980), pp. 80-81.

must say, 'I am Brahman.' "[3] For the Hindu, this monistic experience is "enlightenment."

In Hinduism, then, the goal becomes an inward quest to discover the "true self" who is god. This discovery is made through the practice of yoga (path). John P. Newport defines yoga "as a broad term including any aspect of Hinduism leading to self-liberation or god-realization."[4] Indian philosopher Vishal Mangalwadi states that the purpose of the yoga is to alter the consciousness to attain a higher state of consciousness. This is accomplished through manipulation of the nervous system by utilizing techniques.[5]

Following is a list and short definition of some of the more popular forms of yoga:

Hatha Yoga: salvation through physical exercise—physical manipulation of one's body to create an altered state of consciousness which occurs as a result of the effect of the exercise on the central nervous system.

Japa Yoga: the "mechanical" path to salvation—the repetitious use of a mantra (sacred word), usually the name of a Hindu god or evil spirit. This creates a state whereby the mind is conscious but unaware of anything or any thought. This state is called pure consciousness or transcendental consciousness.

Kundalini Yoga: salvation through the serpent—Hinduism teaches that at the base of the spine is a triangle in which lies the "Kundalini Shakti" (Serpent Power). It is usually dormant but when it is awakened it travels up the spine to the top of the head, passing through six psychic centers called "chakras." As it passes through a chakra, one receives psychic experiences and powers. When it reaches the top chakra, supposedly, the power to perform miracles and achieve liberation is realized.

Tantra Yoga: salvation through sex—Tantra is the way of pleasure and indulgence. Through techniques orgasm is prolonged to achieve unity consciousness or to experience god.

3. Ralph Rath, *The New Age: A Christian Critique* (South Bend, Indiana: Greenlawn Press, 1990), p. 32. Quoting John P. Newport, *Christ and the New Consciousness* (Nashville, Tennessee: Broadman Press, 1978), pp. 14-18.
4. Ibid., p. 34. Quoting Newport, *Christ and the New Consciousness*, p. 18.
5. Ibid. Quoting Vishal Mangalwadi, *Yoga* (Chicago, Cornerstone Press, 1984).

Many practices are crude and disgusting and include worship of sex organs, sex orgies, drinking blood and human semen, and human sacrifice.[6]

To make progress toward self-realization, a Hindu must have a guide or master to whom he submits completely. This spiritual teacher is called a *guru*. Some gurus are looked upon as *avatars*—Hindu gods who are incarnated on earth in times of great need. Another type of guru is a *sad-guru* (perfect master). Unlike the avatar who *descends* from the heavens to earth, the sad-guru is said to *ascend* into the divine while still on earth. This is accomplished by achieving union with god. He is a man-god. The guru's function is to lead each student in a specific spiritual discipline called a *sadhana*. If the discipline is faithfully followed, the student should attain god-realization or a mystic trance. These disciplines include breath regulation, meditation, and concentration.[7]

However, even faithful adherence to a spiritual discipline does not always produce god-realization for the Hindu. *Karma* often interferes. Karma is the Hindu law of retribution which teaches that one's present life is the result of a past action from a former existence. "The present condition of each individual's interior life—how happy he is, how confused or serene . . . is an exact product of what he has wanted and got in the past; and equally, his present thoughts and decisions are determining his future states. Each act he directs upon the world has its equal and opposite reaction on himself."[8] Because of past actions, a soul may need to pass through a series of bodies before it reaches god-consciousness. This process of death and rebirth is known as *reincarnation* or *transmigration*.

Many gurus have come to the United States with their own schools of Hinduism. One such individual is Maharishi Mahesh Yogi who came to the States in 1959. Calling his movement the

---

6. Definition adapted from Rath, *The New Age: A Christian Critique*, pp. 34-37. Rath is quoting from Mangalwadi, *Yoga*.
7. Ibid., p. 33. Quoting from Newport, *Christ and the New Consciousness*, pp. 14-18.
8. Huston Smith, *The Religions of Man* (New York, New York: Harper and Row Perennial Library, 1965), p. 76.

Spiritual Regeneration Movement, the Maharishi soon discovered Americans were not interested in Hinduism. Undaunted, he returned a few years later, changed the name of his organization to one less religious in tone—American Foundation for the Science of Creative Intelligence—and has sold transcendental meditation (TM) as a nonreligious relaxation technique ever since. Though promoted as a secular organization, the TM technique and its accompanying initiation rite are overtly Hindu. The initiation ritual includes worshipping a Hindu deity and the mantra given to the student is the name of a Hindu god.[9] This mantra is repeated over and over again until an altered state of consciousness is achieved. This altered state brings with it a natural peace and sense of well-being. TM attracts thousands of meditation-seeking students every year, many from college campuses and classrooms, and most of whom have no idea they are participating in a Hindu religious rite.

Buddhism

The New Age Movement also borrows liberally from the oriental eastern religion of Buddhism. The Buddhist belief system developed from the personal revelation and enlightenment of Siddhartha Gautama, a Hindu man who lived in India around 500-400 B.C.

Though many stories surround Siddhartha Gautama, legend has it that as a young man he had a series of four visions. In the first vision he saw an old man. In the second vision he saw a sick man; in the third—a corpse; and in the fourth, a wandering holy man. From this, Siddhartha deduced that life involves aging, sickness, and death. The fourth vision indicated to him that he should leave his family and seek religious enlightenment which would free him from life's sufferings.

For six years, Siddhartha wandered as a monk, practicing many forms of asceticism. However, since none of these practices led to enlightenment, he abandoned them. Legend says that one day he decided to meditate under a "bo" tree, vowing not to

---

9. Rath, *The New Age: A Christian Critique*, p. 29-30, 130-134.

leave until he gained enlightenment. After many hours of Hindu meditation, enlightenment came. From then on, he was called Buddha which means "enlightened one" and his insights became known as the Four Noble Truths.

Buddha taught that existence is a continuous cycle of death and rebirth and that karma influences one's present state in life. Buddha believed that as long as an individual remained in the cycle of death and rebirth, he could never be free from pain and suffering. The nature of Buddha's enlightenment was that man can find a release from his sufferings in *nirvana,* a state of total happiness and peace. However, nirvana can only be attained when one completely frees himself from all desire.

To be freed from all desire, Buddha taught that one must follow the Middle Way and the Noble Eightfold Path. The Middle Way is a moderate approach to living which avoids over-indulgence and extreme forms of asceticism. "The Noble Eightfold Path consists of 1) knowledge of the truth; 2) the intention to resist evil; 3) saying nothing to hurt others; 4) respecting life, morality, and property; 5) holding a job that does not injure others; 6) striving to free one's mind from evil; 7) controlling one's feelings and thoughts, and 8) practicing proper forms of concentration."[10]

Buddha's teaching became known as the *dharma.* There are several different schools of Buddhism in existence today. They include the Theraveda, the Mahayana, and the Mantrayana.

Zen

One form of Buddhism that has had a great influence on the New Age Movement, and many Christian communities as well, is Zen, which means "meditation" in Japanese. In the sixth century, Buddhism came to Japan from India by way of China, thus becoming influenced by the Chinese religion of Taoism. The emphasis in Zen is on experience rather than reason. "The goal of Zen is the attainment of a state of spiritual enlightenment called *satori* where the individual realizes that all reality is one (monism). Zen Buddhists believe that intense concentration and

---

10. *Worldbook Encyclopedia, Vol. 2* (Chicago, Illinois: World Book, Inc., 1988), 678.

meditation to empty the mind is the key to achieving satori."[11] This concentration and meditation involves the use of a *koan,* an apparently contradictory riddle which expresses a grcat spiritual truth. "The *koan's* contradictions increase pressure in the trainee's mind until the structures of ordinary reason collapse completely, clearing the way for sudden intuition"[12] (satori).

The satori experience shatters all dualities. It brings about an experience of "oneness which is at once empty because it dismisses all distinctions as inconsequential, and completely full because it spills over to include everything. As the Zennist put the matter, 'All is one, one in none, none is all.' . . . The experiencer has passed beyond the opposites of good and evil, pleasure and pain, preference and rejection . . . each is welcomed in its place."[13] Thus, a true monistic experience has taken place.

It is in this shattering of dualities that the influence of Taoism is most apparent. Taoism teaches the "relativity of all values and, as the correlate of this principle, the identity of contraries."[14] This concept is depicted by the Chinese symbol of *yin* and *yang.*

"This polarity sums up all life's basic oppositions: good-evil, active-passive, positive-negative, light-dark, summer-winter, male-female, etc. But though the principles are in tension, they are not flatly opposed. They complement and counterbalance each other . . . In the end both are resolved in an all-embracing circle, symbol of the final unity of *Tao.* Constantly turning and interchanging places, the opposites are but phases of a revolving wheel . . . It turns and bends back upon itself until the self comes full-circle and knows that at center all things are one."[15]

11. Ibid., *Vol. 21,* p. 604.
12. Smith, *The Religions of Man,* p. 147.
13. Ibid., p. 151.
14. Ibid., p. 211.
15. Ibid.

The influence of Eastern Oriental Religions on the New Age Movement is substantial. Their monistic, pantheistic doctrine is part and parcel of New Age belief. Reincarnation, karma, avatars (also called spirit guides and ascended masters by New Agers), yin and yang, meditation, and enlightenment all find a comfortable home in the New Age expression.

What Does the Catholic Church Say?

The "Declaration On The Relation Of The Church To Non-Christian Religions" from the *Documents of Vatican II* states the Roman Catholic Church's position regarding non-Christian religions including Hinduism and Buddhism:

> The Catholic Church rejects nothing of what is true and holy in these religions. She has a high regard for the manner of life and conduct, the precepts and doctrines which, although differing in many ways from her own teaching, nevertheless often reflect a ray of that truth which enlightens all men. Yet she proclaims and is in duty bound to proclaim without fail, Christ who is the way, the truth and the life (*John* 1:6). In Him, in whom God reconciled all things to Himself (*2 Cor.* 5:18-19), men find the fullness of their religious life.
>
> The Church, therefore, urges her sons to enter with prudence and charity into discussion and collaboration with members of other religions. Let Christians, while witnessing to their own faith and way of life, acknowledge, preserve and encourage the spiritual and moral truths found among non-Christians, also their social life and culture.[16]

While the Church acknowledges that "a ray of that truth which enlightens all men" may be found in non-Christian religions, including Hinduism and Buddhism, and that Catholics are urged "with prudence and charity" to enter into discussion and collaboration with members of these religions, the Declaration does not state that Catholics are free to engage in the religious practices and rituals of these religions, nor adopt aspects of their religious

---

16. Austin P. Flannery, Editor, *Documents of Vatican II*, "Declaration on the Relation of the Church to Non-Christian Religions" (Grand Rapids, Michigan: William B. Eerdmans Publishing Co., 1980), p. 739.

beliefs and philosophies into their own worldview. Instead, it states that Catholics are "duty bound" to proclaim Jesus Christ in whom is found the fullness of revelation, to witness to their own faith and way of life, and to encourage non-Christians with whatever spiritual and moral truth they find among them and in their social life and culture.

Eastern Meditation and Centering Prayer
An Interview with Patricia

Patricia explains her experiences with the world of Eastern Oriental meditation. She compares what she learned there with the Christian use of centering prayer.

Johnnette: Pat, can you share with us how you first became involved in transcendental meditation?

Patricia: I was 19 years old. I was a sophomore in college and it was the Fall of 1973. I had seen some flyers hanging up around campus saying that there was going to be an Information Night. And I was attracted to the flyers and wanted to find out more information. Basically, it was a night when they were selling all of the good things about TM. And it was that night that I signed up and made an appointment to be initiated.

Johnnette: To be initiated. What was that initiation process like?

Patricia: I remember I had to bring an apple, a handkerchief, and a flower. What I remember was coming to the teacher's home. I brought those things, someone greeted me at the door, and I know the room had flowers in it. It also had a picture of Maharishi's guru. It was not a picture of Maharishi himself. It was a picture of the teacher who had taught Maharishi TM. It was set up like an altar. There was a table with a cloth, and this picture and some incense and a candle. And I remember the teacher saying to me that he would say some things in a language that I wouldn't understand and that he was going to kneel down. He told me I was free to kneel down if I wanted to but I didn't have to. And I remember feeling uncomfortable because it did look like an altar. But I still went through with the initiation.

Johnnette: What was the method you were taught for TM?

Patricia: We were taught to get comfortable. We could be sitting in a chair or sitting on the floor. We were to close our eyes, repeat the mantra we were given. I wasn't supposed to pay attention to my breathing, I wasn't supposed to have any thoughts. If I did have thoughts I was supposed to ignore them and to think about the mantra.

Johnnette: Did you practice this meditation on a regular basis?

Patricia: At that time I did. I was to practice it for fifteen minutes in the morning and fifteen minutes in the late afternoon or evening. And then after a period of time you were to meditate for twenty minutes. I was very faithful to the practice for two years—for the rest of my time in college.

Johnnette: What was going on in your life at the time you practiced transcendental meditation?

Patricia: There were a lot of frustrating things going on in my life and at home. And it was an outlet. It was a means of finding a way of relaxing. I think one of the things I realized was that at the time I knew kids who were involved in drugs or who were involved in sexual relationships, and I just knew those things weren't for me. And yet, I wasn't dealing with my problems. I had a lot of pent up anger that I've had to deal with. At the time, TM was a way to deal with it without even admitting it was there.

Johnnette: What types of follow-up activities were there with the transcendental meditation?

Patricia: They have teaching programs that were going on. I attended several of those. They had films that would explain—I can see now how they were explaining an Eastern philosophy. They also had weekends similar to going on a retreat except that you weren't spending time in prayer, you would spend time meditating. At the time I was practicing TM and attending their workshops, I was also attending the Catholic Church to find out more about my faith.

Johnnette: Was there ever a time when you saw transcendental meditation being in conflict with the teachings of your own Catholic faith?

Patricia: Yes, there were several times. They spoke about TM being "the way." And, of course, Jesus is the Way. And I thank God that I did have my Catholic faith and that it was solid so that I could hear these discrepancies.

Johnnette: I know that you have been exposed to centering prayer, Pat. What is your reaction to centering prayer?

Patricia: I remember very well listening to the person giving the lecture on centering prayer and being kind of perturbed because she was using some of the very same words that had been used to describe transcendental meditation. I remember her talking about how important it was to be quiet and to ignore thoughts. I remember her talking about how things would bubble up and it was very good to have these thoughts bubble up.

Johnnette: Was the technique you were offered for centering prayer similar to the technique you were offered for transcendental meditation? Was there any observable difference?

Patricia: No. My experience with TM really matched what was being taught for centering prayer.

Johnnette: From your experience, Pat, what would you say to someone who is searching for the same peace that you were searching for?

Patricia: I guess I would recommend that whatever their problems are they are not too big for God. And to trust that He has a plan for them and He will help them to work through whatever it is that is making their lives difficult.

Questions for Reflection

1. How is the Hindu and Buddhist understanding of reality different from the Christian view?
2. How are the Hindu and Buddhist views of God, man, and salvation different from the Christian perspective?
3. Contrast the Christian perspective of good and evil with that of Buddhism and Taoism.
4. To what extent do I consider it "safe" to implement non-Christian techniques into my life? My prayer life?
5. St. Paul says, "Do not conform yourselves to this age but be transformed by the renewal of your mind, so that you may judge what is God's will, what is good, pleasing, and perfect" (Romans 12:2). What can I do to renew my mind? What standards can I apply to judge what is God's will, what is good, and what is perfect?

Scripture Passages for Meditation

Day One: *Genesis* 1: 26-31
Day Two: *Hebrews* 12: 18-24
Day Three: *Matthew* 16: 13-18
Day Four: *John* 14: 5-6
Day Five: *Hebrews* 13: 8-9
Day Six: *1 Corinthians* 2: 1-5
Day Seven: *Matthew* 6: 22-23

WEEK THREE

"Anyone who loves me will be true to my word, and my Father
will love him; We will come to him and make Our dwelling place
with him."
—*John* 14: 23

Is Centering Prayer Contemplation?

Many people desire to come into a deeper relationship with
God. The way in which we do this is through prayer. The
Catholic Encyclopedia defines prayer as "the raising of the mind
and soul to God."[1] Prayer generally consists of adoration (recognizing the majesty of God, and our own dependence on Him for
all things), praise (honoring God for who He is), thanksgiving
(thanking God for all that He has done for us), and petition (asking God for specific favors and blessings).

Prayer takes many forms but it is most often divided into
two categories—vocal prayer and mental prayer. Vocal prayer
uses words that have been developed beforehand. Examples of
vocal prayer are the Hail Mary, the Our Father, the prayers of
the Holy Sacrifice of the Mass, and the Liturgy of the Hours.
Vocal prayer can be recited alone (private) or with a group
(public). Singing the Liturgy of the Hours and the Holy Mass
are beautiful expressions of public vocal prayer.

While vocal prayer uses predetermined words, mental prayer
is spontaneous and expresses sentiments and emotions that rise
up out of the pray-er's own mind and heart. Many think mental
prayer is only for a select few, primarily for priests and religious;
however, mental prayer is for everyone and should be a part of
every Christian's prayer life. There are two types of mental
prayer—meditation and contemplation.

---

1. Robert C. Broderick, *Catholic Encyclopedia,* (New York, New York: Thomas Nelson
   Publishers, 1976), pp. 485-487.

21

Christian Meditation

"Meditation is that form of mental prayer in which the mind is specially occupied with reflecting on divine things. These prayerful reflections become the means of stimulating the will to make acts of confidence and sorrow, of gratitude and petition, and of adoring love of God."[2]

The Church recommends the use of Sacred Scripture for meditation. The lectio-divina method of meditation is an ancient prayer tradition of the Church. Lectio-divina encourages the pray-er to read a passage of Scripture and ask these questions: "What does this mean contextually and in the culture of the time? What is God saying to me personally through this passage? What is my response to God?" Through lectio-divina, then, we enter into a dialogue with God. We read His Word and hear His Word, and then we formulate a response. (See page xii.)

The great saints of our Faith have also recommended that we use Scripture as a basis for mental prayer. St. Ignatius Loyola suggested that we use our imaginations to place ourselves into a scriptural scene. We imagine ourselves as one of the characters in that scene and dialogue with Jesus about our thoughts, feelings, and emotions. St. Teresa of Avila, the great mystic saint, also advised her nuns to use their imaginations in mental prayer. She particularly suggested that they envision the Passion of Our Lord and be with Him in love during this painful time. St. Teresa herself used the image of Jesus as He was scourged at the pillar. She said this method of mental prayer is very safe and effective.

Contemplation

When our prayer becomes punctuated by impulses of loving sentiments toward God which grow in intensity and frequency, it signals a deepening of our prayer life and becomes preparation for a more intimate loving union with God. It leads us to the second form of mental prayer, contemplation. In this form of mental prayer, "the mind is not so much reasoning about God as looking at God in simple faith and adoration. It may be called the end or

---

2. John A. Hardon, S.J., *The Question and Answer Catholic Catechism* (New York, New York: Doubleday, 1981), p. 317.

purpose of meditation. . . . To contemplate is to see God with the eyes of faith."[3] As in any loving relationship, the more time we spend gazing into the eyes of the beloved, the more in love we become. So too, contemplation leads us into an ever-deepening love of the Beloved. "By depth here we mean a knowing loving that we cannot produce but only receive. . . . It is a wordless awareness and love that we of ourselves cannot initiate or pro-long."[4] We enter into a loving communion with the triune God, a communion that is infused and comes from no effort of our own. All faculties of our being are caught up, suspended if you will, in the loving embrace of the Holy Trinity. When this type of prayer persists, it can lead to mystical union or spiritual marriage—a "secret union" with God that takes place in the very center of our soul.

The first stage of contemplation is called "acquired contempla-tion." It flows from meditation. As St. Francis de Sales says, "Prayer is called meditation until it has produced the honey of devotion; after that it changes into contemplation." Acquired contemplation begins when meditation yields to a simplistic gaze on the object of love—God. It is called "acquired" because the pray-er is still active at this stage. He *utilizes* meditation, *quiets*, the senses, and *yields* to devotion. Also called simplified affec-tive prayer, acquired contemplation prepares the soul to receive infused contemplation should God grant it.

Infused contemplation, on the other hand, is pure gift, a special grace of the Holy Spirit. It does not depend upon our efforts, can-not be produced by our efforts, and is freely given by God to whomever He wishes. While we can be disposed to receive this gift, as the saints suggest, through Christian meditation, acquired contemplation, and living a life of virtue, techniques are rendered useless. "Repeatedly, (St.) Teresa insists that contemplative prayer is divinely produced. She calls this prayer even in its deli-cate beginnings 'supernatural,' meaning by this term what we now intend with the word infused, that is, poured in by God.

---

3. Ibid., p. 318.
4. Thomas Dubay, S.M., *Fire Within* (San Francisco, California: Ignatius Press, 1989) p. 57.

Entering into the prayer of quiet or that of union whenever she wanted it 'was out of the question'."[5]

Is Centering Prayer Contemplation?

One prayer method or technique that is gaining great popularity in prayer communities, parishes, and groups throughout the country is centering prayer. By this term we are referring to that prayer which concentrates on emptying the mind of thought through the repetition of a single word. We are not referring to prayer that centers on Jesus Christ and our relationship with Him. The former is often presented as a *technique* that *leads* to contemplation or as contemplation itself.

Several differences separate centering prayer from what we know traditionally to be contemplative prayer. First of all, contemplative prayer is usually the fruit of a long life of prayer. While God can and will give such a favor to whomever He chooses, it seems that He usually gives the favor of contemplative prayer to those who have made progress in living a life of virtue for some time. That is why St. Teresa of Avila advises those who aspire to a life of prayer to first begin to live a life of virtue. Those who promote centering prayer, however, "promise any Christian at any stage access to contemplative prayer."[6] This raises concern for two reasons. One, it implies a manipulation of the favors of God through practicing a technique. Two, it suggests that a technique can obtain for the practitioner the same fruit as a life of holiness.

Meditation on Scripture or on things of the divine (Christian meditation) usually is the prelude to the contemplative prayer experience. God then moves the pray-er into a deeper awareness of His presence and infuses him with His love. Centering prayer does not include meditation on Scripture. Instead, it advises the pray-er to select a word (monosyllabic is best) to express His "intentionality" which is loving union with God. He is to return to this word any time a distraction or thought (holy or otherwise)

---

5. Ibid., p. 59. quoting from *The Life* from *The Collected Works of St. Teresa, Vol. 1,* Washington Province of Discalced Carmelites, 1976.

6. Dan DeCelles, "Centering Prayer Meets the Vatican", Part One, (*New Heaven/New Earth,* March, 1990).

occurs in his mind. In short, he is to empty himself of thought or suspend his thinking process.

This, too, raises some questions. One, if centering prayer is to lead us to contemplation and if contemplation is the experience of the loving presence of God, how can this occur if we reject His overtures through loving impulses or thoughts of Him? Two, St. Teresa warns that if we try to suspend intellectual operations on our own (before God gives the grace of infused contemplation), we can drive ourselves silly ("Unless His Majesty has begun to suspend our faculties, I cannot understand how we are to stop thinking, without doing ourselves more harm than good . . . ." [*The Interior Castle,* fourth mansion, chapter 3]).

This emptying of the mind by using a monosyllabic word is often explained as a preparatory step for infused contemplation. As such, it is likened to acquired contemplation. However, in explaining acquired contemplation, Father Reginald Garrigou-Lagrange, O.P. states, "If by acquired contemplation we mean a prayer distinct from simplified affective prayer, *in which the intellect is totally absorbed by its object and in which we place ourselves by the suppression of all rational activity, we thereby not only create a degree of prayer unknown to St. Teresa and St. John of the Cross, but we likewise oppose their explicit teaching.* In fact, St. Teresa repeatedly opposes the total suppression of discourse and the movement of thought as long as one has not received infused contemplation (*Life,* chap. 12; *The Interior Castle,* fourth mansion, chap. 3. St. John of the Cross, *The Ascent of Mount Carmel,* Bk. II, chap. 15)."[7]

More Questions

Proponents of centering prayer often say that it is the ancient prayer form of the Church, tying it in to the anonymous work, *The Cloud of Unknowing.* Others place it in the same category as the Jesus Prayer. (Repeating, "Lord Jesus Christ, only Son of the Living God, have mercy on me a sinner.") Still others say that

---

7. Father Reginald Garrigou-Lagrange, O.P., *The Three Ages of the Interior Life, Vol. II* (St. Louis, Missouri: B. Herder Book Co., 1948. Reprinted by TAN Books and Publishers, Inc., Rockford, Illinois, 1989), p. 311. Italics in text my own for emphasis.

John Cassian's interview with Abbot Isaac in *Conferences* describes a prayer method that is essentially the same as centering prayer. In all of these cases, the similarities are ambiguous. The author of *The Cloud of Unknowing* states "that techniques and methods are ultimately useless for awakening contemplative love."[8] The Jesus Prayer expresses a complete thought, thereby putting a thought into our mind. It also places the pray-er in right relationship with Our Lord as one who is a sinner in need of God's mercy. Further, it tells us who Jesus Christ is—the Son of the Living God. Rather than using the Jesus Prayer to dismiss thought, the pray-er is to meditate on the profound mystery expressed by the words, eventually making them the substance of his life. Finally, differences exist between centering prayer and the prayer method of Abbot Isaac. ("O God, make speed to save me; O Lord, make haste to help me.") Like the Jesus Prayer, this formula places us in proper relationship to God who saves us; and its content, too, is crucial to the prayer.[9]

Yet another consideration of the centering prayer method is what is to take place during the prayer time. For the major proponents of centering prayer, this is to be a time for the "dismantling of the false self." The false self is the result of all the psychological and emotional baggage we have been carrying with us throughout our lives. Its root, according to centering prayer proponents, is original sin which is defined as ". . . a way of describing the human condition, which is the universal experience of coming to full reflective self-consciousness without the certitude of personal union with God."[10] For the centering prayer practitioner, regular practice of "contemplative" prayer sets in motion a dynamism of "divine psychotherapy, organically designed for each of us, to empty out our unconscious and free us from the obstacles to the free flow of grace in our minds, emotions, and

---

8. *The Cloud of Unknowing,* edited by William Johnston (Garden City, New York: Doubleday, 1973), p. 92.
9. Dan DeCelles, "Centering Prayer and Cassian's *Conferences*" (New Heaven/New Earth, February, 1991), pp. 11-12.
10. Kerry J. Koller, "But Is It Prayer?", (*New Heaven/New Earth,* February, 1991), p. 12, quoting Father Thomas Keating.

bodies."[11] As this false self is dismantled, we come to see our true Self, the center of which, so say proponents, is God—"God and our true Self are not separate. Though we are not God, God and our true Self are the same thing."[12]

In Christian spirituality, the motivating factor for prayer and meditation is the individual's knowledge of his total dependence upon God and his need for a savior. He recognizes that he is a sinner who is predisposed to err as a result of original sin. Centering prayer, however, seems to redefine sin as a cultural and environmental problem which is resolved through the centering prayer process by the dismantling of the false self. One might then ask, "Is a savior necessary?" In his article about centering prayer, "But Is It Prayer?" Kerry J. Koller states, "One of the truest and deepest things about me is that I am a sinner and inclined to sin at a very deep level. This is part of my character, part of the real me, the self in one of its truest manifestations. I come before (God) aware of my own sin and ask forgiveness, His mercy, and His grace to change. It is not a method for getting some leverage on God and making Him do what I want, nor, as the teachers would have it, some psychological exercise for transforming myself into godlike beatitude."[13]

Finally, centering prayer bears an astonishing resemblance to transcendental meditation, both in form and in its hoped for results of psychological and emotional freedom.[14] Some of the major proponents of centering prayer have been instructed in Eastern meditation techniques by Hindu and Buddhist teachers. In addition, some proponents of centering prayer mention the value of integrating Eastern meditation techniques and practices, especially TM, into our prayer forms. And many of the terms and definitions used in centering prayer are the same or similar to many concepts expressed in Eastern Oriental religions.

---

11. Thomas Keating, *Open Mind, Open Heart* (Amity, New York: Amity House, 1986), p. 93.
12. Koller, "But Is It Prayer?", p. 13, quoting Father Thomas Keating.
13. Koller, p. 13.
14. For a good study on the similarities of transcendental meditation and centering prayer, read Father Finbarr Flanagan's article, "Centering Prayer: Transcendental Meditation for the Christian Market," in the May/June, 1991 issue of *Faith and Renewal*.

As we have seen, the documents of Vatican II state that "the Catholic Church rejects nothing of what is true and holy in non-Christian religions."[15] However, was it the intention of the Council Fathers that we should follow the prayer patterns of a non-Christian people? Since the Hindu concept of God is very different from the Christian view, is it possible that by practicing these techniques, techniques specifically developed to lead to an awareness of a monistic god, we can be seduced away from our own Christian understanding of God? Could we begin to perceive God as only immanent, one with our "true Self?" Would we then be tempted to see ourselves as God? Finally, what about the mystical state that is achieved as a result of these practices? Is it a state of union with the triune God which brings the peace that surpasses understanding? Or is it instead the natural rest which is the result of transcendental meditation? Or a mystical state from an unholy source?

The questions and the considerations raised in this discussion, point to the need for further study into the nature and effect of centering prayer. Perhaps only the time-tested fruit of such a practice can answer them. Ultimately, does the practice lead us closer to the God of the Christian, or away from Him?

Centering Prayer: A Pastoral Perspective
An Interview with Father Emile Lafranz, S.J.

Father Emile Lafranz, S.J. was director of The Center of Jesus the Lord in New Orleans, Louisiana, for twenty years. In addition to traveling throughout the United States preaching about the Holy Spirit and living a life in the Lord, much of Father Lafranz's time was spent in giving pastoral counselling and spiritual direction to the numbers of people who came to the Center. On Ascension Thursday, May 25, 1995, Father Emile Lafranz went home to be with Our Lord.

Johnnette: Before we talk about prayer, it is important for us to start with a definition. What is prayer?

---

15. Flannery, *Documents of Vatican II*, p. 739.

Father Lafranz: St. Teresa talks about prayer as conversation with God. It's the faith that enables us to enter into a relationship with the Father in the Son through the Holy Spirit.

Johnnette: What is centering prayer?

Father Lafranz: I need to be very careful here. Prayer will have through the grace of God the normal progression of simplifying. And there is a centering on Jesus Christ which must always be encouraged. A personal relationship with Him. A centering likewise on the word of God that makes Jesus so present to us. But there is a *technique* of prayer that has become quite popular over the last twenty years and that's called centering prayer. And I would say that it is simply transcendental meditation in a Christian dress.

Johnnette: Father, let's talk about the roots of this centering prayer technique. Where does it come from?

Father Lafranz: I honestly believe it comes from Hinduism. And it is an attempt to reach an altered state of consciousness. A type of mysticism, not Christian mysticism, but a natural mysticism in which there is a feeling of a peace. And many people get into it and they realize there *is* a change that is happening. But I would say this is not due to the power of the Holy Spirit. I believe it's something that can likewise introduce a person to an evil spirit. Why I say this is that when we go into the void, we need to be extremely cautious. We don't go unprotected. Evil spirits *can* touch us if we don't have our minds and hearts guarded. As we're told in the sixth chapter of St. Paul's letter to the Ephesians, "Put on the armor of God." What concerns me so much is that a technique is being used to come into contact with God, a technique that will automatically produce mysticism. Union with God is a grace, a gift of God. We cannot create this experience. It is a gift of God. I would say we need to be extremely cautious. When we open ourselves, what spirit is coming in? The Holy Spirit? Is it an evil spirit? That is why I would definitely say Christians need to recognize that first and foremost we need to come with the protection of the Holy Spirit, recognize that the focus has to be on God. Not upon ourselves. I find that this type of prayer actually has the individual looking more and more into himself. He becomes more and more self conscious. The reason I would say this is by it's very nature, coming from transcendental meditation, or Hinduism, their understanding of God is very different from the Christian understanding of God.

Johnnette: Share with us, Father, What is that difference?

Father Lafranz: Hinduism believes in a pantheistic awareness of God. All is God. And to become more and more conscious of this relatedness with the "is-ness" of all creation is the goal of Hinduism. It's simply something that is passive. For Christians, we believe that God is different from matter. God is separate from matter. The creator is not the creature. God is involved in our lives. He is present to us at the deepest core of our being. But we're not God. The fallacy of the New Age is that it is a proclamation that we are God. That was the first heresy. The first temptation, "You will be like God."

Johnnette: Father, we're talking about a technique, and I know that one of the things that concerns me about centering prayer is that it is sometimes stated that centering prayer is a means of coming into contemplative prayer. And sometimes it's even stated that centering prayer *is* contemplative prayer. What is contemplative prayer?

Father Lafranz: Contemplative prayer is first of all a gift from God. It's an infused experience of God's presence with us through faith and through love. And likewise as a result of the gifts of the Holy Spirit we become more aware of God's presence to us. The normal progression of the Christian is to grow in the contemplative awareness of God. It's an infused gift of God. In other words, we can't create it. We can humbly go before God, in repentance we can turn our lives over to God, and after a period of time we can grow in a deeper understanding of God. But it's a process. It doesn't happen overnight. I believe that what is happening today is people are being told to go into centering prayer and in an instant you will be holy.

Notice the cross is absent in centering prayer, and there can be no growth without the cross.

Johnnette: I have found that many people who are involved in centering prayer are truly longing for a deeper relationship with God in their lives. How can we begin this relationship with God?

Father Lafranz: I would say that is the quest of most individuals, for God. As Amos puts it, "The hunger is not for bread alone but for the word of God." And there is a greater need to experience the holy within our churches. I believe we need to create an atmosphere where we come into a deeper relatedness with God. Where we enable people through openness to the power of the Holy Spirit to come to a personal encounter, a personal experience of God. I believe the answer to the New Age is really the New Pentecost, the power of the Holy Spirit. I believe in our day the Lord definitely led Pope John XXIII to experience that the solution to the problems of the day is being in the new Pentecost, a new empowerment of the Holy Spirit. I believe this is so intimately connected to true prayer. I believe the gifts of the Holy Spirit enable us to come to a new encounter with God, for example, the gift of tongues, such a beautiful way for us to enter into contact with God, to seek His face. Not to simply go into a void and to let whatever comes come, but a personal seeking for God.

Questions for Reflection

1. In what ways does the Christian understanding of meditation and contemplation differ from that of Eastern Oriental Mysticism?
2. To what extent may I have been exposed to or influenced by non-Christian meditation techniques?
3. To what extent am I truly convinced that a life of prayer is a necessity for me? How does the Word of God enhance my relationship with Him and impact my daily life?
4. Is my prayer time conformed with the great tradition of prayer that we have in our Church or am I mixing it with influences from other areas?

Scripture Passages for Meditation

Day One: *Isaiah* 45: 19
Day Two: *Hebrews* 4: 12
Day Three: *Isaiah* 11: 2-3
Day Four: *2 Corinthians* 6: 14-18, 7: 1
Day Five: *2 Corinthians* 10: 3-5
Day Six: *Matthew* 6: 6, 17-18
Day Seven: *Colossians* 1: 17-19

WEEK FOUR

"Live on in me, as I do in you. No more than a branch can bear fruit of itself apart from the vine, can you bear fruit apart from me. I am the vine, you are the branches. He who lives in me and I in him, will produce abundantly, for apart from me you can do nothing."
—*John* 15: 4-5

Mysticism

Authentic mysticism is a participation in the supernatural life of God. This participation is a pure gift from God. God invites; we respond. Through the Sacrament of Baptism, we are all invited to participate in the supernatural life. As the grace of Baptism is received into our souls, we become members of Christ's mystical body. This "membership" brings with it the indwelling presence of the Holy Spirit of God.

The Action of the Holy Spirit

It is through the activity of the Holy Spirit within us that our life in God grows and develops. As Saint Hilary states in his treatise, *On the Trinity,* "We receive the Spirit of Truth so that we can know the things of God." To explain this relationship, he compares it to the senses of the body:

> In order to grasp this, consider how useless the faculties of the human body would become if they were denied their exercise. Our eyes cannot fulfill their task without light, either natural or artificial; our ears cannot react without sound vibrations, and in the absence of any odor our nostrils are ignorant of their function. Not that these senses would lose their own nature if they were not used; rather, they demand objects of experience in order to function. It is the same with the human soul. Unless it absorbs the gift of the Spirit through faith, the mind has the ability to know God but lacks the light necessary for that knowledge.

It is through the action of the Holy Spirit in our lives that we come to know God. Jesus tells His disciples, *"When the Paraclete comes, the Spirit of Truth who comes from the Father . . . He will bear witness on my behalf . . . He will guide you to all truth. He will not speak on His own, but will speak only what He hears, and will announce to you the things to come. In doing this He will give glory to me because He will receive from me what He will announce to you"* (*John* 15: 26; 16: 13-14).

Through the Word of God, participation in the Holy Sacrifice of the Mass, frequent reception of the Sacraments of Holy Eucharist and Reconciliation, and private prayer, our life in the Spirit grows and develops and we begin to "know the things of God." Gradually, we begin to notice the transforming effect of God's grace operating within us. Interiorly, this grace is manifested by a hunger and longing for God. Exteriorly, we experience a change in our behavior, our thoughts, our ideas. A desire for holiness and virtue begins to fill our life. We cease living for our own natural wants and desires, and begin to live a life centered on God and His will for us. We desire to live the love of God—God loving through us. And thus, we reach the summit of Christian life—true mysticism. "Ultimately, the substance of the highest Christian mysticism entirely consists in the knowledge and love of God attaining here below a supereminent purity and transparency to grace."[1]

Mystical Phenomena

But what of mystical phenomena? According to Louis Bouyer, "Neither visions, nor ecstasies, nor raptures, nor anything of the kind constitute an integral part of (Christian) mysticism."[2] While God may use such phenomena in the progress of certain souls, these phenomena are not only unessential to progress in the spiritual life, but, as stated by St. Teresa of Avila and St. John of the Cross, such experiences suggest an embryonic stage of the mystical life. "It should be added, not only that the mystics canonized

---

1. Louis Bouyer, *Introduction to Spirituality,* (New York, New York: Desclee Company, 1961), p. 300.
2. Ibid., p. 299.

by the Church have all more or less gone beyond experiences like this, but also that many, and among them the greatest, have never known anything of the kind."[3]

Bouyer suggests that we must take a very cautious approach to such phenomena should it occur. "Not only should we not attach ourselves to such things, not only should we keep a very critical mind with regard to what may be truly supernatural about the origin of such experiences, but, even when we have the most certain reasons for thinking that in anything like this we are not the plaything of the devil or of our own imaginings, we must still positively will to go beyond them."[4] Authentic mysticism always leaves the pray-er with a great desire for the God of consolation rather than the consolation of God.

Misconception #1: Psychology = Spiritual Life

Today, two errors are prevalent with regard to mysticism. The first is the tendency to "psychologize" spiritual life. This results in reducing the spiritual to various states of consciousness produced by psychological means. In Christian mysticism, the underlying reality is relationship with God. "It follows that no spirituality— Christian spirituality least of all . . . [because of] the importance to it of the personal relationship with God—can, therefore, be adequately studied by means of a purely psychological analysis . . . there can be no question of interpreting . . . the Christian spiritual life [without] the God Who dominates it: the God Who speaks to us through Christ in the Church. The steps, the aspirations, even the movements of such a spirituality become incomprehensible if we neglect what is their moving force."[5]

Misconception #2: Syncretism

Syncretism is the second error common in modern spirituality. Bouyer suggests that this error flows from the first. If we assume that the spiritual life is simply a matter of psychology, then we can assume that "religious experience" is the same everywhere

---

3. Ibid., pp. 299-300.
4. Ibid., p. 299.
5. Ibid., p. 18.

for everyone and "that the character of the mystical experience is completely indifferent to particular dogmatic formulations."[6] This can lead one to believe that the spiritual experience of the Hindu, the American Indian, the Buddhist, the Christian are all the same. Indeed, in much New Age literature today we read that all paths lead to God. Spirituality is simply seen as an underground river which can be accessed by many different wells.

Still another problem arises with syncretism and the psychologizing of religion. If psychology reduces the spiritual life to various levels of consciousness, then individuals seeking the spiritual may use these levels as erroneous indicators of spiritual experience. This is what we see happening with many individuals, Christians as well as New Agers, who claim mystical experiences. Through self-induced trances and other activities that lead to an altered state of consciousness, a mystical union is achieved which is mistaken for union with God. Most damaging is that in many cases, what is experienced is a mystical monism, where all things, including the individual himself, seem to be interrelated by a cosmic life force or energy force (all is one). The New Age claim is that this "force" is God and since it pervades man as well, then man is god. This new awareness is called christ-consciousness and man's godhood is the true self, or the higher self.

Syncretism leads yet to another problem. Discernment. If one believes that all spiritual experience is essentially the same, then there is no need to "test" the spirit. Bouyer humorously recalls the story of the hermit to whom Satan appeared as an angel of light. Satan told the solitary soul that he had been sent from Heaven to assure the monk of his great progress in the interior life. The man replied, "You must be mistaken; it is certainly to some other person that you have been sent!"[7] St. John reminds us, *"Beloved, do not trust every spirit, but put the spirits to a test to see if they belong to God. . . . This is how you can recognize God's Spirit: every spirit that acknowledges Jesus Christ come in the flesh belongs to God"* (*1 John* 4:1-2). Satan is a great counterfeiter and can use mystical experiences to lead a soul astray.

---

6. Ibid., p. 19.
7. Ibid., p. 299.

Authentic Mysticism

Authentic mysticism is never self-induced. It is always the action of the Holy Spirit within us. God invites; we respond. As Bouyer states, "No mysticism, no Christian mysticism in any case, is worthy of the name if it pretends to be the product of any method whatever which a man might master by the appropriate technique."[8] In addition, in authentic mysticism, never is the distinction blurred between the Creator Who is God, and the created, who is man.

According to Thomas Dubay, S.M. in his book, *Fire Within*, all authentic Christian mystics insist "that God and the individual remain unambiguously two distinct beings: the one is not absorbed and lost in the Other."[9] Finally, the true mystic is not concerned about the experience of mysticism. The true mystic's attention is completely riveted on the Object of the experience— God Himself. As such, authentic mystical experience can only flow from a life of faith.

Louis Bouyer states, "This is the meaning that mysticism should hold for us. It is . . . the truths of the Gospel, the realities of the sacramental life which the Christian accepts by faith, and makes his own by charity."[10]

True Mysticism: A Gift From God
An Interview with Father Edmund Sylvia

Father Edmund Sylvia is a Holy Cross Father who teaches in the Graduate Counseling Department at the Franciscan University of Steubenville. He is also a mental health counselor at the University's counseling center.

Johnnette: What is mystical experience?

Father Sylvia: Mystical experience is a participation in relationship with God. That is our Christian definition of what mystical experience ought to be. There are other kinds of mystical experi-

---

8. Ibid., p. 288.
9. Dubay, *Fire Within*, p. 7.
10. Bouyer, *Introduction to Spirituality*, p. 304.

ences, though. There is what's called natural mysticism. That's the kind of thing where one would experience peace, serenity, a certain calm. Certainly, being around nature would induce this feeling, this communion. There is also the mysticism that comes with monism, the belief that all is one. This way, in which a person can actually lose the boundaries of the ego and merge with this cosmic ocean, is often spoken about in the New Age Movement. And there is also demonic suggestion that can pose as a mystical experience.

Johnnette: How do we distinguish Christian mysticism from these other kinds of mysticism?

Father Sylvia: This is where discernment is so important. What's called discernment of spirits is very much at the heart of the theology of St. Ignatius of Loyola. A very important gift for the people of God to be able to distinguish what is really going on there. Is it the Holy Spirit? Or is it created spirit that can be either angelic or demonic? Or is it again human spirit that is communing with our spirit?

Johnnette: In that discernment process, what would be some guidelines that we could use?

Father Sylvia: First, of course, is the Word of God. How does this experience line up with the presentation of the Scriptures and how the Church has taught those Scriptures? The Church's teaching is meant to be a guide to us in this way. It calls us to try and put these things into a right moral perspective and helps us understand the limits of coming at this just from emotionality. And there is also the importance of good spiritual direction. None of the mystics or those whose names we would readily recognize were without this very important component of spiritual direction. By the time one has come to this union with God that is called mystical prayer, this guidance along the journey is of critical importance.

Johnnette: Is mystical experience meant only for a few or is it meant for all of us?

Father Sylvia: Because it is in fact representative of the gift of God, of His very Self to us, His desire to commune with us, this is really the call of all Christians. It comes by virtue of our baptism. We are all baptized into Christ—made into sons and daughters. What son or daughter would the Father not want to commune with? He wants to be able to communicate Himself. This heavenly dialogue He has designed and it is meant to enrich every heart.

False Mysticism:
Experience From An Unholy Source
An Interview with Paul Yunger

Paul fell away from the Catholic Church at the early age of eleven years old. But, as a young man he became rooted again. This time in occultism. Paul feels, "If Satan can convince you he doesn't exist, he's won half his battle."

Johnnette: Can you tell us how you became involved in occultism?

Paul: Part of it came in the late 60's or early 70's. We had moved to Florida from Ohio. At that time I had a brother who had gone out to see a medium, and over a period of time he more or less got the whole family involved, one step at a time.

Johnnette: In what aspect of occultism did you become the most proficient?

Paul: Proficient, my best area was in teaching. I could teach people to be better than I was. I was good in astrology. I did a small amount of mediumship. I was good at teaching ESP.

Johnnette: Tell us a little about your experience of being a medium. What was it like?

Paul: I was very lightly into that area. I think probably my will to be in control was what kept me from going deeper into that.

Essentially you allow someone else to take over control of your body and speak through you. Today they call it channeling. In my opinion there is no difference between the two.

Johnnette: How would you allow this presence to come in?

Paul: Basically you go through different relaxation techniques for a beginner. And then you would have the person open himself up to what we would call his "spirit guide." Kind of like the occult version of the guardian angel, so to speak. And then over a period of time many people were able to go deeper and become what we would call a "dead trance medium." This is someone who is completely unconscious and the other spirit completely takes over and you notice changes in the voice pattern and things along that line.

Johnnette: Is that what happened to you?

Paul: I never became a dead trance medium. As I said earlier, my desire to be in control was too great. I would simply hear the voices in my head and then relate what I heard.

Johnnette: There's a deception involved in all of this. What is the deception?

Paul: The deception is that what they're doing is good. But what they are really doing is leading you away from Christ. The easiest person to fool is an intelligent educated person because they are trained to think in a certain pattern. And once they are thinking in that pattern, you can fool them easily.

Johnnette: How did you begin to reinvolve yourself with Jesus Christ.

Paul: The Lord had His hand on me no matter how far away I was. I think one of the things that led me to the Catholic Church aside from the fact that my parents were in it years ago, was the consistency. I read all of the documents of Vatican II. I read the documents of the Council of Trent. And their argumentation was excellent and made good sense. I remember I finally came back to the Church on an Ash Wednesday and it was a matter of that decision process, not an emotional experience.

Johnnette: What is the safety net, Paul, that keeps us on the right path?

Paul: Keeping your eyes on what the Church is saying so that you follow what the Church teaches. Long term, watching what the Church has said over a number of years. Reading the lives of the saints such as Teresa or John of the Cross and Little Therese, helps set a pattern for us. Channeling and those things, while they seem to have answers, if you compare them to what the Church teaches, you'll find a definite difference.

Johnnette: In retrospect, Paul, what do you regret the most about your occult involvement?

Paul: The fact that I led people down the path. Like I said, I was a good teacher. And as a good teacher I had a number of people I would work with and help them along that path. In that area, I have the greatest regret. That I led those people further away from Jesus Christ.

Johnnette: What one word would you say to those who are beginning to dabble in the occult?

Paul: It's going to fool you. Satan wants to hook you—make it look like you are getting everything you want, but let you dangling just a little more so that he can hook you further. On the other hand, Jesus Christ wants to fill you up fully.

Questions for Reflection

1. What potential dangers exist when we apply a syncretistic approach to prayer?
2. In Matthew 7, verse 17, Jesus says, "Any sound tree bears good fruit, while a decayed tree bears bad fruit." What is the fruit of my prayer time?
3. To what extent do I find myself relying more on the grace of God and less on my own efforts?
4. One of the gifts of the Holy Spirit is the gift of discernment. This gift begins to take shape and form in us as our minds are renewed in Christ. As we read Scripture, receive the Sacraments with revitalized faith, and enter into a life of prayer, we begin to evaluate and judge our daily circumstances and interactions with the wisdom of the Holy Spirit. Situations and decisions are weighed against the standard of Holy Scripture and the teachings of the Roman Catholic Church. Another manifestation of this gift is *discerning of spirits*. This gift is given in the moment in which it is needed and occurs when the Holy Spirit enlightens us instantly to know what spirit is operating within an individual or a situation.
   a) In light of this explanation, consider an example of this gift being manifested in your own life.
   b) How can this gift be useful in evaluating our own thoughts, actions, and motivations?
   c) St. Ignatius of Loyola emphasized the importance of discerning of spirits during prayer. Why should this gift be exercised during our prayer time?
   d) The gift of discernment is one of the defenses Our Lord gives us against the attacks of the Evil One. How can this gift be an invaluable aid on our spiritual walk?

Scripture Passages for Meditation

Day One: *John* 3: 4-8
Day Two: *Ephesians* 1: 3-6
Day Three: *John* 15: 4-5
Day Four: *Ephesians* 3: 14-20
Day Five: *Titus* 2: 11-14
Day Six: *John* 14: 1-6
Day Seven: *John* 14: 23

> *"I tell you all this so that no one may delude you with specious arguments . . . . See to it that no one deceives you through any empty, seductive philosophy that follows mere human traditions, a philosophy based on cosmic powers rather than on Christ."*
> —*Colossians* 2: 4, 8

Gnosticism and Occultism

The New Age Movement is really not new. Rather, it is a repackaging of all of the old heresies. Monism, pantheism, and gnosticism all find expression in the New Age Movement. While monism states that all is one and pantheism believes that the One is "God," gnosticism claims that man's spirit is a "divine spark" which has been imprisoned in matter. The goal of the gnostic is to be "awakened" from ignorance of his divine essence to gnosis (knowledge), an "awakening" typically gained through magical and occult practices. The word "occult" means "secret" or "concealed" and alludes to a power that can be experienced through a hidden wisdom. The gnostic's salvation lies in this esoteric knowledge and its power to transform him. The seeker is usually inducted into this gnosis through a process of initiation rites and rituals. These rites and rituals are often cloaked in secrecy and the initiated is sworn through oaths to keep the secret.

Gnosticism versus Christianity

Gnosticism contrasts sharply with Christianity. First of all, gnosticism is esoteric—hidden and meant for an elite few. Christianity, on the other hand, is exoteric—open and meant for everybody. The gnostic sees his salvation flowing from a hidden wisdom and his ability to gain this knowledge. However, for the Christian, salvation comes through Jesus Christ and our cooperation with the redemptive grace He secured for us through His passion and death. We receive this grace, not through the occult and magical practices of the gnostic, but through our baptism into His Mystical Body and a life of faith.

Historically, gnosticism is rooted in the ancient mystery religions of the Far East and Egypt. Gnosticism undermined orthodox Church teaching during the first four centuries of Christianity. The Church formally refuted gnosticism at the Council of Nicaea in 325 A.D. However, it still has its advocates today. Elaine Pagel's book, *The Gnostic Gospels,* claims that the early gnostics were a persecuted minority whose teachings were suppressed for political and ecclesiastical reasons rather than for theological ones. In spite of the fact that modern scholarship supports the historical credibility of the canonical Gospels, *The Gnostic Gospels* won the National Book Critics award in 1979.[1]

One popular story among the New Age set claims that Jesus traveled to the East and was initiated into gnostic and esoteric mysteries. This supposedly took place during the eighteen years of his life which are not related in Scripture. He is pictured by them as an adept yogi (a Siddha) who attained enlightenment and set out to teach others about their own potential powers to control themselves and the world around them. New Agers separate the historical Jesus Christ from the christ consciousness—that state of realized godhood supposedly attainable by all. To them Jesus is not the God-man, but the man-god, one whose godhood was realized.[2]

Gnostic Organizations and a Common Theme

One gnostic/occult organization that has had particular influence on New Age thinking is the Theosophical Society. Its founder, Helena Petrovna Blavatsky, has been credited as the "godmother of the New Age Movement."[3] Founded by Blavatsky in 1875, Theosophy is a blend of occultism and the Eastern mysticism of Hinduism and Buddhism. Blavatsky's ideas and

1. Groothuis, *Unmasking the New Age,* pp. 144-149.
2. Ibid., p. 146.
3. Nina Easton, "Shirley MacLaine's Mysticism for the Masses," (*Los Angeles Times Magazine,* Sept. 6, 1987), p. 10. Quoted by Russell Chandler, *Understanding the New Age* (Dallas, Texas: Word Publishing, 1988), p. 47.

writings are claimed to have come through "ascended masters," highly evolved spirit beings who impart wisdom and knowledge.

The Theosophical Society believes that genuine occultism's "primary concern is with the universal laws governing all natural phenomena."[4] Theosophy teaches that "There is one homogenous divine substance-principle from which the visible world arises . . . Everything in the universe, throughout all its kingdoms, is conscious, i.e., endowed with a consciousness of its own kind and on its own plane of perception . . . Every individual is fundamentally identified with the universal Oversoul and passes through cycles of incarnation in accordance with the law of cause and effect."[5]

Another theme that runs through theosophic literature is the dawning of a New World Order and the coming of a world-wide religious teacher. Annie Besant, Blavatsky's successor to the presidency of the Theosophical Society, attempted to usher in a new messiah in 1929. However, the young Indian chosen and groomed for the job, Jiddu Krishnamurti, rejected his status and broke away from the movement.

The themes of a New World Order and one world religion are especially prevalent in the writings of Alice Bailey, who followed Besant as president of the Theosophical Society. She eventually started her own occult organization, Lucis Trust (originally Lucifer Trust). Bailey's writings were supposedly received telepathically from a spirit entity she called Djwhal Khul, "The Tibetan." Throughout her books, she gives specific instructions for implementing "the Plan"—a one world government and a one-world religion. Bailey's organization, Lucis Trust, sponsors World Goodwill, a political lobby group headquartered on United Nations Plaza.

Another gnostic/occult organization that echoes the one-world

---

4. Information taken from the pamphlet, "The Historical Basis of Modern Theosophy," published by the Theosophical Society of America, Box 270, Wheaton, Illinois 60189.

5. Ibid. With regard to the theosophical concept that everything in the universe has a consciousness of its own, it is interesting to note that *The New Age Catalogue* (Carol Iozzi, et al. New York: Doubleday, Island Publishing Co., 1988, pg. 20), states this about quartz crystals: *Each crystal is unique, has its own personality and experiences, and is to become a working partner with humans so that we might serve each other's evolution.*

government and one-world religion theme is Freemasonry. Virulently anti-Catholic and anti-Christian, Freemasonry membership is opposed by many Christian denominations. According to Paul A. Fisher, researcher and author, "It is evident that international Freemasonry historically has been a revolutionary world-wide movement organized to advance Kabbalistic Gnosticism; to undermine and, if possible, to destroy Christianity; to infuse Masonic philosophy into key government structures; and to subvert any government which does not comport with Masonic principles."[6]

Indeed, from 1941-1971, traditional Judeo-Christian values were removed from American public schools and public life in general. These are the same years in American history that Masons dominated the Supreme Court bench.[7] Throughout history, the Catholic Church has voiced loud opposition to Freemasonry. As late as 1983, Joseph Cardinal Ratzinger issued a Declaration which states that "Masonic membership is a serious sin that denies to Catholics 'the right to approach Holy Communion.'"[8]

Gnosticism Within

Unfortunately, gnosticism is not only an important component in gnostic organizations and in New Age thinking; it is also an essential element in the theology of many radical Catholic feminists and theologians.[9] Donna Steichen, author of *Ungodly Rage: The Hidden Face of Catholic Feminism,* states, "Among America's educated elites, including Catholic elites, religion is now understood as a symbol for personal opinion, faith as a metaphor for imagination, mysticism as altered consciousness however achieved . . . The religious impulse is turned away from the transcendent Creator to center on subjective consciousness as

---

6. Paul A. Fisher, *Behind the Lodge Door* (Bowie, Maryland: Shield Publishing, Inc., 1989), p. 16. Fisher's comment is based upon his research which included reading every issue of the Masonic journal from the years 1921-1981. This journal is called, interestingly enough, *New Age.*
7. Ibid., pp. 1-2.
8. Ibid., p. 201.
9. Donna Steichen, *Ungodly Rage: The Hidden Face of Catholic Feminism* (San Francisco, California: Ignatius Press, 1991), pp. 161-165.

the source of spiritual truth, the principle of moral judgment, the object of veneration and service and the explanation for the persistence of traditional belief among the simple peasantry. . . On that landscape, within the province of the modernist theological scholarship that defines religion as a psychological phenomenon, implicitly gnostic religious feminism overlaps an explicitly gnostic New Age Movement."[10]

Freemasonry: A Secret Society
An Interview with William Still

William Still is the author of "**New World Order: The Ancient Plan of Secret Societies.**"

Johnnette: Freemasonry is a system of initiation into degrees. Tell us about the first three degrees.

William: In the first three degrees of masonry we see in the first degree the mason has to swear to slit the throat of any fellow mason who reveals the secrets of masonry. In the second degree he has to agree to cut the heart out while it is still beating of the unfortunate mason who reveals the secrets of masonry. And in the third degree he has to swear to disembowel the unfortunate mason who reveals the secrets. Now, Jesus told us not to swear any oaths at all much less horrible blood oaths.

Johnnette: What happens in the higher degrees?

William: In the fourth, fifth, and sixth degrees we see masonry take on a different character entirely. The mason must swear to help get any fellow mason off of any crime, murder and treason not excepted. This is the backbone of the "good old boy" system as it used to be called in the South.

Johnnette: In your book, William, you talk about an "inner" and an "outer" doctrine of masonry. What is this doctrine?

William: This is the way they keep masons in the dark, at least

---

10. Ibid., p. 193.

lower level masons, about what the real purposes of the order are. If you're going to have a successful secret organization, especially in the United States, it has to be one that brings in the pillars of society and holds them. Now usually the only way to do this is to convince them that they are doing something good for the world or the organization or their locality. Never convince them that they're doing something bad. This is the outer doctrine, the deception that you're doing something good for the world in general by joining masonry. Whereas, if you study the history of secret societies, and masonry in particular, you see that their goals are anti-Christian and in fact anti-nationalistic although masons in the first three degrees are told just the opposite.

Johnnette: What would you define as the goals of freemasonry?

William: Well, the goals of freemasonry are basically three essential points—the political, the religious, the economic—masonry in today's world specializes in the religious aspect of this, however. You have to look at masonry, especially in the United States, as a system of steps, initiated steps designed to take the Christian from Christianity up the ladder of masonry towards deism. In the deist type of philosophy, God doesn't exist in the present day world. He existed to begin the world initially but He doesn't exist in the present day world. Therefore you can throw out the concept of absolute morality, you can throw out the concept of Jesus, of salvation. And this is the basis of all the concepts of the New Age Movement and secret societies.

Johnnette: You talk about ancient secret societies. Are they all connected?

William: Yes, essentially. They all have at their core the same concept, "How do we bring the nations of the world to this new order, to this internationalist system, whereby peace and brotherhood and harmony can be brought on perpetually by mankind?" And, of course, those of us who know the Bible know that it will not be mankind who brings on that state of peace and harmony.

Johnnette: Since the goal of freemasonry is the elimination of Christianity, what does that mean for those of us who are Christian?

William: We're going to be doing spiritual battle right up until the end. We can't accept this New World Order concept. It's based on the concept of internationalism and that's not a good thing. We have to continue to base our world on the concept of nationalism. Only in that way can nations be held in a relative state of freedom.

Johnnette: Now that you have researched this and written your book what is the word that you would share with the American public?

William: You have to continue to build up Christian values, family values. You have to oppose masonry as a pagan, anti-Christian system. Mankind through his own efforts is not going to bring on a world of peace and harmony. Just the opposite. He is going to bring on wars and rumors of wars and eventually the reign of the anti-Christ.

Questions for Reflection

1. Gnosticism is enticing because it stimulates the intellect. Have I fallen prey to it in any way? How clearly do I see my salvation flowing from the merits of Jesus' passion and death?
2. What is the difference between Christian wisdom and the wisdom of the gnostic?
3. Many ecology organizations and associations as well as humanitarian groups support the New Age agenda. As a responsible Christian, I should be aware of the political agenda of groups and organizations to which I contribute in any way. Are there any organizations that I support which promote New Age ideas and agendas? How should I react?
4. In Matthew's Gospel, chapter 13, verses 4-23, Jesus tells us the parable of the seed. In what ways am I like the seed that landed on good soil? How do I display characteristics of the other seeds described?

Scripture Passages for Meditation

Day One: *Colossians* 2: 4-8
Day Two: *Ephesians* 5: 6-17
Day Three: *Matthew* 7: 13-14
Day Four: *Matthew* 7: 24-27
Day Five: *1 Corinthians* 1: 18-25
Day Six: *Ephesians* 6: 10-17
Day Seven: *Galatians* 1: 6-9

WEEK SIX

> *"In the past, when you did not acknowledge God, you served as slaves to gods who are not really divine. Now that you have come to know God . . . how can you return to those powerless, worthless, natural elements to which you seem willing to enslave yourselves once more?"*
>
> —*Galatians* 4: 8-9

Neo-Paganism and Creation Spirituality

New Age pantheism and monism find expression in many forms. Included among these expressions is neo-paganism. According to *Harper's Encyclopedia of Mystical and Paranormal Experience,* neo-paganism is "an eclectic modern movement primarily concerned with revived and reconstructed pre-Christian nature religions and mystery traditions."[1] *Harper's Encyclopedia* states "Neo-pagans view creation as an unbroken and interconnected whole, and hold all life equally sacred."[2] While there are three general principles of neo-paganism—polytheism, pantheism, and animism—"not all neo-pagans believe in all three principles."[3]

Neo-pagans hold that the Divine Force is immanent[4] and recog-

---

1. Rosemary Ellen Guiley, *Harper's Encyclopedia of Mystical and Paranormal Experience* (New York, New York: Harper Collins Publishers, 1991), p. 401.
2. Ibid.
3. Ibid. **ANIMISM**—any religion in which the souls of dead people and spirits of nature have an important role. These religions also believe that spirits exist in trees, flowers, hills, water, rocks, etc. and therefore worship these parts of nature. For definitions of **POLYTHEISM** and **PANTHEISM**, see Week 2, Footnote 2.
4. In these belief systems, God is considered to be inherent in creation. He has no transcendent quality (above and independent of the physical universe). As Christians, we believe that God is separate and distinct from His creation but that He preserves the world through His almighty power. When we speak of God's immanence in a Christian sense, we are speaking of His indwelling presence as described by Jesus in *John* 14:26. God dwells in the hearts of those who love Jesus Christ through the Presence of the Holy Spirit within them (*1 John* 4:15-16; *1 Corinthians* 3:16). The Holy Spirit consoles, guides, and transforms lovers of Christ and thereby gives them a foretaste of Heaven. However, even though we share closely in the life of God through the indwelling presence of the Holy Spirit, He remains God and we remain creatures. John

nize both its female and male aspects—The Goddess and the Horned God. The Goddess is seen as the most powerful entity of the Divine Force and is revered in all of her manifestations—Creator, Destroyer, Moon, Great Mother. Neo-pagans often picture her as Diana, a trinity called the Triple Goddess, who is manifested in the three persons of Virgin, Mother, Crone. In addition, the Goddess is seen as Gaia, the living Mother Earth, and many neo-pagan rituals and rites are celebrated in conjunction with the fertility cycles of nature.

Neo-pagan rituals are often performed "skyclad" (nude) and generally liberal attitudes toward sex prevail throughout neo-paganism. The practice of magic and divination, and the development of psychic skills is central to the neo-pagan expression. Based on the birth-death-rebirth cycle of nature (Wheel of Rebirth), neo-pagans hold to the concept of reincarnation. Neo-pagans draw from many sources including shamanism, Native American spirituality, Eastern religions, Celtic and Druid practices, and African religions.

Wicca

Neo-paganism's consummate form of current expression is in wicca (witchcraft). Today's witches come together in covens for eight traditional seasonal holidays called "sabbats." These sabbats celebrate the Wheel of Rebirth which wiccans believe is made possible by the union of the Goddess and Horned God. These celebrations include much chanting, drumming, and dancing to achieve a state of ecstasy. Often, the Horned God or Goddess is "drawn down" through trance channeling.[5] October 31 (Halloween) is the high holy day of wicca. As with other neo-pagan beliefs, the major focus of wicca is on magic, divination, and psychic abilities.

In their covens, witches "cast the circle" and raise "the cone of power." The circle is constructed according to ritual and is con-

---

A. Hardon, S.J. states in *The Catholic Catechism,* "Historic Christianity is unique among the religions of the world in recognizing on faith what mere human reason tends to see as contradictory: that God is both infinitely distant from us in His essence and intimately close to us by His presence."

5. Ibid., p. 402.

sidered a sacred space that creates a gateway to the gods. It symbolizes wholeness, oneness, the cosmos, the womb of Mother Earth, and the Wheel of Rebirth. Dances (often skyclad) are performed in the circle and wiccans believe transcendent levels of consciousness can be attained within its sphere. The cone of power is raised within the circle. It is seen as a force field of psychic energy raised for magical purposes. Holding hands, the witches begin to dance in a ring and chant to raise the power. The power is visualized as a cone, the base of which is the circle and the apex of which extends into infinity or is pictured as a person or symbolic image. The shape of the witch's hat symbolizes the circle and the cone of power.

When the energy reaches a peak level, the power is released to accomplish its goal, usually the casting of a spell. Witches maintain that they only use their magic for good purposes (white magic). However, they do acknowledge the existence of black magic and some do believe in the judicious use of curses.[6]

Creation Spirituality

Within Catholic circles, one movement which is closely identified with neo-paganism and wicca is the creation spirituality of Matthew Fox, director of the Institute for Culture and Creation Spirituality at Holy Names College in Oakland, California. *Harper's* states that "Creation spirituality advocates the rebirth of an earthly ecstatic mysticism that reveres the feminine principle, sexuality, passion, play, prophecy, creativity, and the divine child within . . ."[7]

Fox holds to "panentheism," a concept which states that God is in everything and everything is in God. He speaks of the "original blessing" of creation instead of original sin claiming that while he does not deny original sin, he believes that dualism, the separation of body and spirit, is the sin behind the sin. In his book *The Coming of the Cosmic Christ,* he depicts Mother Earth as the symbol of the crucified cosmic Christ and urges his disciples to search, not for the Jesus of Nazareth (a search which he

6. Ibid., pp. 108-109, 118, 649.
7. Ibid., pp. 122-124

claims is "Christolatry"), but rather for the christ who is in each of us.[8] At his institute he collaborates with Starhawk (Miriam Simos), his faculty witch.

Donna Steichen, author of *Ungodly Rage: The Hidden Face of Catholic Feminism,* states that while Fox has not been taken seriously by theologians,[9] he has had a profound effect on women religious whose careers within the Church include "campus ministry, youth ministry, retreat centers, feminist organizations, Catholic schools and colleges, and other parish and diocesan positions, including pastorates."[10]

Because his writings and teachings border on the heretical, Fox was silenced for one year by the Vatican, effective December 15, 1988. In 1992, he was asked by his provincial to return to community life in Chicago to facilitate an on-going discussion about his writings. He refused. On February 22, 1993, he was officially dismissed from the Dominican Order by the Undersecretary of the Congregation for Institutes of Consecrated Life and Societies of Apostolic Life.

A Priest's Perspective of Neo-Paganism
An Interview with Father Paul Desmaris

Father Paul Desmaris is Director of the Cult Awareness Network for the Diocese of Providence in Rhode Island.

Johnnette: What do you make of some of the neo-pagan claims that we can contact the spirit-world?

Father Desmaris: Obviously there is a lot of fraud. Anybody can create a deep dark voice or fake a trance. But there are also claims that are true. Throughout the entire Old Testament through the New Testament, and into the Acts of Apostles there are a lot of instances where people are in contact with the dead. Yahweh warns the Israelites in *Deuteronomy* to stay away from people

---

8. Matthew Fox, O.P., *The Coming of the Cosmic Christ: The Healing of Mother Earth and the Birth of Global Renaissance* (San Francisco, CA: Harper & Row, 1988).
9. Steichen, *Ungodly Rage,* p. 222.
10. Ibid., p. 223.

who are channelers of the spirits of the dead. The Jews in the Old Testament took it seriously. Jesus in the New Testament took it seriously. And the apostles had to encounter that in the Acts of the Apostles. Even today the Church still warns people that spirits are real, that the spirit world is real, that we have to be aware of it, that we have to watch out for it and that we have to stay away from it.

Johnnette: When people begin to enter into occult practices, what typically begins to happen to them?

Father Desmaris: Most enter it out of curiosity. Most enter it because they've heard from friends about fortune-tellers, palmists who can predict the future with accuracy. Some of them are fraudulent, some hire detectives to research your background before you come to them. However, some of them are true mediums. Some of them know how to use a Ouija board, know how to use tarot cards to contact spirits to predict people's future.

Johnnette: What is the danger of entering into these types of occult practices?

Father Desmaris: Yahweh is very clear in the Old Testament to stay away from these practices. First of all what it does it really cuts the person off from the power of God. God is a very jealous God who calls us into relationship with *Him*. Occultism calls us into relationship with the spirit-world—it cuts us off from relationship with God. Secondly, it opens people up to spiritual harassment. Those spirits that have entered into their life stay. And while they think it is fun, a parlor game, they have nevertheless opened a door to a spirit-world. Those people who then become harassed find it very difficult to keep their relationship with God. And they find it very difficult to pray, to read Scripture, to attend Mass. I worked with a mother and her daughter. The mother was a practicing wiccan, practicing witch, who was teaching her daughter these practices. The daughter came to my youth center to read people's fortunes. I pulled her aside and told her how inappropriate this was. We went into the chapel to talk about this and pray. And she could not physically stay in that room. In the Presence of the Eucharist, she was forced to get up and leave because she could not be in the Presence of the Eucharist. There is a real spiritual harassment that takes place, an oppression that takes place, when people contact the spirit-world and when they invite the spirit-world into their life.

Johnnette: I know in your work in the Diocese of Providence, you encounter this quite a bit. How do you begin to deal with the oppression someone may be under.

Father Desmaris: The first thing I do is to begin to pray with that person and ask that person if they sincerely want to repent, to change their life around, to bring back the power of God into their life. If they're willing to do that, the first thing I do is to begin to set up prayer. The Body of Christ is so important. I have people who will put that person on a prayer list and begin to pray for that person. The Sacrament of Reconciliation is important. The Sacrament of the Eucharist is important. That person needs to repent. To say to God, "I am sorry for inviting this into my life." To receive the Eucharist. Depending on the degree of oppression, of involvement, and after they have gone through the basic steps, I may suggest that they go through deliverance ministry. Now people may get scared at deliverance ministry. But, it's a way of discerning through the Holy Spirit to what degree this person has been involved in the spirit-world and to what degree they are being harassed by spirits in their life. Is it the everyday temptation that we all go through, or is it indeed true spiritual oppression or in some cases possession.

Johnnette: You mentioned parlor games earlier and I know that at sleep-overs many children play with Ouija boards and other occult games. Is there any safe level of involvement in the occult?

Father Desmaris: No, the parlor games that they play—tarot, Ouija boards—are clear doors to the spirit-world. There are in occult practices specific doors that will open you to the spirit-world, to the world of the dead. And those are two clear doors that people enter through. I have talked to—I have lost track of the number of teenagers I have talked to—but they will say that in playing the Ouija, in contacting a spirit, there is a dramatic change in their life afterwards. One girl put it this way, "After playing that game, there was a cold dark evil presence in my life and I knew it wasn't good." And she wasn't able to shake that presence at all. She said, "It haunts me. It haunts my dreams. It haunts my spirituality with God and my relationship with other people."

Johnnette: How do we know if what we are experiencing is coming from God or from some other source?

Father Desmaris: In occultism it is so important for a person to control the ritual or control the chant of a prayer, whatever they do to call up the spirit, they control it. Ritual involves you being able to perform the ceremony, the ritual, the chant correctly. If you veer off at all then you do not empower that spirit to come forth. Revelation of God to a person is God's free gift to that person. In occultism, the person is trying to be in control, to be the master of the spirit-world, to tell the spirit what to do, we control it. In our faith tradition, God reaching out to us is God's free gift. We have no control over what God gifts us with or blesses us with. And that's the real difference. We cannot manipulate God. God blesses us freely.

Questions for Reflection

1. Many neo-pagans have a great concern for nature and are active in ecological organizations and programs. While there is merit in their concern, how does their motivation, view of nature, and man's responsibility toward it contrast with the Christian perspective.
2. How are the beliefs and activities of neo-paganism in conflict with Christianity?
3. The practice of magic (white or black) is expressly forbidden by Scripture and the teachings of the Roman Catholic Church. How can its practice put our faith in God in jeopardy?
4. Idolatry takes many forms. Is there anything in my life that I place before God (money, power, material things, sex, education, job)? In what way(s) can I begin to restore balance?

Scripture Passages for Meditation

Day One: *Galatians* 4: 8-9
Day Two: *Exodus* 20: 2-6
Day Three: *Romans* 1: 21-23
Day Four: *Colossians* 1: 15-16
Day Five: *Philippians* 4: 8-9
Day Six: *Isaiah* 5: 20-21
Day Seven: *Philippians* 2: 6-8

WEEK SEVEN

*"They will be treacherous, reckless, pompous, lovers of pleasure
rather than of God as they make a pretense of religion but negate
its power. Stay clear of them. It is such as these who worm their
way into homes and make captives of silly women burdened with
sins and driven by desires of many kinds, always learning but
never able to reach a knowledge of the truth."*
—2 Timothy 3: 4-7

Wicca and Catholic Feminism

Though witches are generally associated with the cultural past,
witchcraft is a growing trend in our culture today. To break with
the stereotypes of the past, the Old English term "wicca" is used
to refer to the craft. But like their predecessors, today's witches
come together in covens to cast the circle, raise the cone of
power, and send it forth to do its work. Today, they also invoke
the goddess within.

In neo-pagan fashion, contemporary witches are worshippers
of nature and have a special reverence for the ancient goddess
religions. According to Douglas Groothuis in his book,
Unmasking the New Age, "interest in the ancient Goddess religion ranges from those motivated to psychologically reform the
Western male-dominated psyche with the potent symbolism and
mythology of the ancients, to those who make Goddess worship a
religious practice, often aligning it with feminist concerns . . .
Goddess enthusiasts usually advocate either the superiority of
women or some kind of androgenous ideal."[1]

Within the Catholic Church in America, many radical feminists have adopted the "Mother Goddess" of wicca in protest of a
masculine hierarchy, natural or supernatural. They see goddess
worship as the antidote to patriarchal religion—a religion they
believe suppresses woman and her power. Underscoring this

---

1. Groothuis, *Unmasking the New Age,* p. 135.

position, Donna Steichen in her book, *Ungodly Rage: The Hidden Face of Catholic Feminism,* quotes Sister Madonna Kolbenschlag, feminist, as saying: "A conversion to matriarchal imagery is often the first and most necessary step in the 'exorcism' of 'God as Father.' "[2]

But exorcising God as Father is not their ultimate goal. Steichen continues, "The 'Mother Goddess' of feminist witchcraft is intended to be a transitional symbol, weaning women from the understanding of God as transcendent Trinity to a concept of the Divine as an essentially immanent and mutable Universal Consciousness, not far removed from pantheism."[3] The goal, then, of feminist wicca is to use the concept of "Mother Goddess" as a ploy to lead women away from the Judeo-Christian concept of God as wholly Other, to the ultimate pantheistic belief that everything is God, including themselves.

Though hardly Catholic in the traditional sense, radical Catholic feminists remain a part of the Church in the hope of "transforming" it from within. Many of them occupy middle management positions within parishes and dioceses, having under their jurisdiction responsibilities as varied as religious education programs, retreat houses, peace and justice programs, and pastoral leadership. Within these capacities, they function as "change agents," individuals intent on propagating and proliferating their own agenda.

Types of Feminism

However, not all Catholic feminism is radical in nature. The Reverend M. Francis Mannion identifies five types of feminism active within the Catholic Church today. In an article entitled, "The Church and the Voices of Feminism," (*America,* October 5, 1991, pp. 212 ff.), he outlines those types:

> The first kind of feminism, which I call "affirmative," generally corresponds to the more "conservative" strand . . .
> Affirmative feminism represents the stance of Catholic

---

2. Steichen, *Ungodly Rage,* p. 92.
3. Ibid., p. 74.

women who wish literally to affirm the church in the traditional place it has accorded women. Affirmative feminism finds strong inspiration in the theology of womanhood set forth by Pope John Paul II and the writings of Hans Urs von Balthasar, Louis Bouyer and Manfred Hauke . . . The conservative feminism with which Catholic affirmative feminism is allied is strongly anti-abortion and opposes those social trends that detach sexuality from marriage and procreation.

"Corrective" feminism, the second type, would be regarded as less "conservative" than the first, yet it shares many of the fundamental convictions and concerns of affirmative feminism. It espouses a deep respect for Catholic tradition, as well as for Catholic culture and family life, even as it criticizes distortions and gender bias in the historical treatment of women . . . This type of feminism normally excludes the possibility of women's ordination. However, the appropriateness of women in other liturgical ministries is recognized and affirmed, as is the entry of women into the world of theology and leadership roles in diocesan administration and parish ministry . . . "Corrective" feminism originates theologically in the recognition of Pope John XXIII in his encyclical "Pacem in Terris" (Peace on Earth [1963]) that a new role for women in the modern world constitutes one of the three most important "signs of the times."

The third type, "reformist" feminism, is very much a product of the mainstream American feminism known as liberal or equity feminism that developed in the 1960's . . . In Catholic reformist feminism, there is a strong conviction of the need to reshape the fundamental structures and doctrines of the church to allow for the participation of women in all ecclesiastical roles, including ordained ministry. Gender-inclusive "vertical" God-language is freely used and encouraged in this approach.

Reconstructive Catholic feminism has as its agenda a thorough dismantling and restructuring of the church in order to recreate new religious communities that are radically egalitarian and non-hierarchical. It has little interest in the ordination of women, viewing ordination as part of the oppressive and power-conserving mechanism of a male hierarchy. This type of feminism tends to regard the Catholic Church and Christianity in general as so deeply and intrinsically sexist, racist and classist that they can only be redeemed by something approaching a revolution . . . The new religious synthesis would include elements from ancient goddess spirituality and non-Christian religions. The ritual style of reconstructive feminism is highly innovative and experimental and habitually generates new feminist "scriptures" and religious symbols. Edwina Sandy's famous sculpture of a female crucified "Christ" (Christa) is paradigmatic of reconstructive feminist spirituality . . . It has significant New Age attachments and often incorporates Native American spiritualities. Matthew Fox, O.P.,[4] and the Oakland-based Institute for Culture and Creation Spirituality are generally associated with reconstructive feminism.

"Separatist" feminism, the fifth type . . . has given up any expectation that the inherited social system is reformable. Accordingly, it holds that women as a group must withdraw to live in a systemically separate world and seek to neutralize the traditional male-engendered world . . . In its relation to Catholicism, separatist feminism is made up of mostly post-Christian women who have separated themselves from the church and Christianity in general, believing both to be irreformable, destructive of authentic womanhood and incompatible with feminist visions and goals . . . It may seem questionable to describe separatist feminism as "church-related." Yet, post-Christian feminists are by definition concerned with Christian ideas, institutions and influences, even if in a fundamentally negative way. They also wield a profound influence on reconstructive feminism . . . More often, however, women in this group unite around a religious symbol system focused on subversive women's activities in history, ancient goddess religion and the European tradition of witchcraft, which the modern Wicca movement recalls and celebrates.[5]

---

4. This article was published before Matthew Fox was officially dismissed from the Dominican Order on February 22, 1993.
5. Reverend M. Francis Mannion, "The Church and the Voices of Feminism," (America, October 5, 1991), pp. 213-216, 228.

From A Researcher's Point of View:
Who Are These Radicals?
An Interview with Donna Steichen

Donna Steichen is author of the book **Ungodly Rage: The Hidden Face of Catholic Feminism.** *Her interest in this area began when she investigated a women's gathering where a ritual dance was performed. She says, "There was a group of several hundred women . . . and they had a brass cauldron in the middle of the floor with smoking incense and they did the spiral dance around it. And chanted chants and called on goddesses. It was the most astonishing thing I ever saw!" Following is a compilation of two interviews with Donna.*

Johnnette: Donna, what is gnosticism?

Donna: Gnosticism has a long history. Essentially it is defined that the way to salvation is secret knowledge. The gnostic is the one who possesses this knowledge. The knowledge or divine revelation is within—no outside authority.

Johnnette: Can you define for us, what is paganism?

Donna: The original kind of paganism that was genuine was largely nature worship, worship of unknown forces. It was genuine—primitive peoples were doing their best to find God. The paganism we find today, or the kind we associate with witchcraft and these other manifestations, is really neo-paganism—a new invention that takes from what they think old witchcraft may have been, or wish it had been, and from other practices—theosophy, psychology—and pull it into a new kind of ritualized religious practice.

Johnnette: I know that in researching for your book you had a chance to observe lots of these rituals. What do they look like and what are these people doing?

Donna: I've seen them dance around trees. I saw a group dance around a soft fabric image of a woman about twelve feet tall. I was told of a group in California that danced around a tree and the tree died! But circle dancing is usually a part of it and calling on gods and goddesses by name.

Johnnette: As I read through your book I was surprised by what you were sharing about Catholic feminists. Who are they and what are their number?

Donna: It's hard to estimate how many there are. Shockingly large numbers come to their conferences—three thousand, four thousand. Whether it's the same three or four thousand who go around to all of the conferences, I'm not sure, but I see increasing evidence of their influence at the parish level all over the country.

Johnnette: What is the search? What are they looking for in all of this?

Donna: Well, I think that some of them are searching for faith. Something to center their lives around. I think the leaders, however, are revolutionaries. I think they're trying to destroy the Church. Among the leaders of the Catholic feminists, I believe as far as I can tell, it's a revolutionary movement that doesn't have too much to do with belief. However, what they use is snatches of everything. It certainly draws on theosophy; Jung is very popular, especially the idea that you don't fight the evils to which you are inclined, but that you incorporate them into your nature as a means of wholeness. There's a lot of humanistic psychology—the sense that all of the answers are within you and you don't have to get them from the outside. And transpersonal psychology which is so new agey I don't know if it has any existence outside of that. Anyhow, transpersonal psychology teaches that you create your own reality. So if you are in a bad situation, you put yourself there.

Johnnette: One strain of this neo-paganism that seems to be taking prayer communities and parishes by storm is the creation spirituality of Matthew Fox. What is creation spirituality?

Donna: Creation spirituality is a very popular form of false spirituality within the Catholic churches which hinges on the reduction of original sin. Basically creation spirituality is a declaration that says creation is good and it has been a mistake to dwell on original sin. It seems to me that it is hardly news that creation is good since that is right there at the beginning of Genesis, but the tone of Matthew Fox when he talks about it is that no one has ever thought about this before. And he's very much opposed to the teaching of original sin. If you pin him down he won't deny there's original sin—he may say that homophobia is original sin or dualism is original sin. But the system of creation spirituality it seems is that it appeals to people who may have been afflicted by guilt—maybe with reason, maybe without reason—but it seems to relieve them of their guilt because all you have to do is take good care of trees. There doesn't seem to be any obligation to personal moral conduct, only this ecology focus. But then it goes on from there to assimilate witchcraft, a little voodoo, and lots of Jung, and all of the strange things that are going on—all of the new agey things that are going on.

Johnnette: On the ecology focus, do you see this drive in our society today toward ecology and protection of the earth as an indicator of this same type of thinking?

Donna: Oh, it's so fashionable you can't turn around without bumping into it in some form or other. Of course taking care of the environment is a good thing within reason, but it's not a religion. And the creation spirituality approach to it and much neo-paganism is that the earth is god, is goddess, Gaia. And even Matthew Fox says the earth is Christ crucified, the cosmic christ crucified. There are people, including nuns, who are followers of this stuff who have given up wearing crosses around their necks in favor of little globes as a symbol of the cosmic christ.

Johnnette: If you take away original sin, as Matthew Fox proposes to do in creation spirituality, then there is no need for a Redeemer.

Donna: Oh yes, that's absolutely true. There is no need for a Redeemer. And Fox goes so far as to condemn what he calls "christolotry," the worship of Christ.

Johnnette: You say that he sees the crucified Christ as creation . . .

Donna: Well, the cosmic christ is what he refers to all the time, but he makes it quite clear that it is not Jesus Christ. He's talking about something else. It's the life force or energy in the universe and he says we have to put away this focus on Jesus of Nazareth—that's christolotry—and we have to instead worship this cosmic christ which is everything. It's really another manifestation of immanence. All of these things, all the neo-paganism things, everything, as far as I can see, their central problem is that they reject a transcendent God. A God who is objectively "other" than us. And they're only willing to recognize an immanent god.

Johnnette: You say this is getting into our churches. How is this happening?

Donna: It's the church middle management. That's who it is. It's many nuns and ex-nuns, and not just women but men too, the professional people within the Church.

Johnnette: What positions would they occupy?

Donna: Lots of diocesan offices. Possibly directors of education in parishes. The influence is certainly evident in catechetics. They are in a lot of retreat centers, anything to do with retreats, to the point where one would hesitate to go on a retreat unless one knew the retreat master.

Johnnette: Let's say that someone wants to determine if this is going on in their own parish. What types of things would indicate that this is the case?

Donna: Certainly, turning away from anything that is clearly and unequivocally Catholic. Jesus Christ, Jesus of Nazareth, Jesus as Redeemer, original sin, a turning away from this to anything that is more equivocal. Ecology-centered—I think you certainly have to watch for that.

Johnnette: We hear these phrases and the words you are using to describe this movement, and it sounds so wholly other. What about the hierarchy of the Church? Why is this allowed to exist?

Donna: The feminists have been very influential with the hierarchy in the United States. Most people have at least heard news articles about the Women's Ordination Conference which is one of the early feminist organizations, Catholic feminists. What they said they were campaigning for originally was ordination. The Catholic Bishop's Conference set up a two or three year dialogue with feminist leaders through Women's Ordination Conference. And the whole campaign to write this pastoral letter on women's concerns came out of this dialogue with feminists. That's one of the reasons I think the letter has so little to do with the concerns of ordinary Catholic laywomen.

Johnnette: In what way is this movement spiritually lethal?

Donna: One way is that it is destructive to the faith of those involved even if they are drawn in gradually. It's destructive because it is an alternative religion. Cardinal Ratzinger has said it is a different religion they are creating. It's also destructive to the faith of the children they come in contact with. It's one of the things that concerns me the most. And not necessarily that the children will buy it all and become new agers, but that the children will think this is Catholicism and they will reject it. And thousands of them, millions of them, are drifting away from the Church. It also opens the danger of actual demonic possession. While it's not Satanism, if they are calling on spirits and contacting spirits, these spirits are probably demons. Certainly angels are not going to be working against Jesus. Things like channeling are really dangerous.

Johnnette: What should we do if we suspect that this is taking place in our parish. Can we do anything about it?

Donna: We should follow the New Testament prescription. First go and talk privately with someone who is doing something wrong. Go with a second person if they don't respond. And finally, go over their heads if they still don't respond. But, in my experience and the experiences that people report to me, it hasn't been very effective. I just think in most situations today, people are far better off if they teach their children catechetics at home and not rely on parish programs.

Questions for Reflection

1. How does feminism play a part in the New Age Movement?
2. According to Father Mannion's categories of feminism, with which group am I most comfortable?
3. What does femininity mean to me? What do I see as the role of women today? How has my culture shaped my perspective of women?
4. Throughout the Bible we find many examples of holy women who had a positive impact on their culture and remained faithful to the One True God. Consider Esther, Ruth, Deborah, Judith, Anna, Mary Magdalene, and Martha. What characteristics do I see in them? How can all men and women follow their examples in daily living?
5. What is my opinion of the Blessed Virgin Mary as a woman? Refer to scriptural passages about the Blessed Virgin Mary. How does she exhibit strength, courage, and leadership? How can I reflect these qualities in my own life?

Scripture Passages for Meditation

Day One: *2 Timothy* 3: 1-7
Day Two: *Matthew* 7: 15-20
Day Three: *Mark* 13: 21-23
Day Four: *1 Timothy* 4: 6-10
Day Five: *Luke* 1: 46-55
Day Six: *John* 4: 4-24
Day Seven: *Luke* 7: 36-50

WEEK EIGHT

"Do not practice divination or soothsaying . . . Do not go to mediums or consult fortune-tellers, for you will be defiled by them. I, the Lord, am your God."
—*Leviticus* 19: 26, 31

Occult Practices

Even a cursory look through the New Age section at most secular bookstores reveals that occultism is a major stream of the New Age Movement. Occult practices are intended not only to lead the New Ager to esoteric wisdom, but also to convince him through successful application that he has gained the power for which he searches. Through occult practices, the New Ager hopes to manipulate the powers of the universe to conform with his own wants, desires, and needs.[1]

Once relegated to carnival mid-ways and sideshows, occultism has become mainstream. Police agencies consult psychics for clues, doctors advise patients to visualize themselves well, and even White House occupants consult astrologers! In newspapers and magazines, articles about out-of-body experiences and astral projection are not hard to find. Movie-makers and television producers have moved occult experiences out of the realm of science fiction and into the plausible. Cartoons and children's literature have been affected as have some elementary school textbooks.[2]

---

1. Manipulation of the powers of the universe is also the classical definition for "magic."
2. Deborah Mendenhall, "Nightmarish Textbooks Await Your Kids," (*Citizens, Vol. 4, No. 9,* September 17, 1990, Focus on the Family). This article examines a textbook series published by Harcourt Brace Jovanovich of Orlando, Florida, called *Impressions,* for use in language arts and reading classes, first through sixth grades. Some versions of this series contain highly questionable themes including witchcraft and the occult with graphic illustrations and descriptions. One of the student workbooks that accompanies the fourth grade reader, *Cross the Golden River,* teaches the children to cast spells. Consider this quote: *This spell creates a blast of lightning that shoots from the caster's hand . . . It is effective against virtually all living creatures that have no magical defenses.* Additionally, the teacher resource book suggests activities that have the children write their own spells: *Tell the children that a magician has cast a spell on some children . . . Have them work in pairs to write the magic spell the magician used. Have*

Some of the most common occult practices are tarot card reading, palmistry, numerology, aura reading, the Ouija board, astrology charts, and all other aspects of divination including the casting of spells. Other occult practices such as seances, channeling, automatic writing, and psychic readings directly invoke the assistance of spirits.

The Enneagram

Unfortunately, practices and techniques rooted in occultism can be found in some Catholic retreat houses, workshops, seminars, and conferences. One such technique is the Enneagram. This technique is sometimes presented as a psychological tool for knowing oneself better or as a method of spiritual direction.

Monsignor William B. Smith, writing in the March, 1993, issue of "Homiletic and Pastoral Review," answers a question submitted to him by a reader who has noticed the widespread acceptance of the Enneagram. Here is his response:

> First, what is the Enneagram? The term "Enneagram" is a compound of the Greek word "ennea," meaning "nine" and the suffix "gram" meaning a drawing. It is a geometric figure of lines that touch or cross. The Enneagram is a circular diagram on which nine personality types are systematically represented at nine equi-distant points on the circumference. Lines connect various points to each other.
>
> It is this diagram itself which is the Enneagram, and it is used as a psychological tool of self discovery. Each of the nine personality types (numbered 1 through 9) is described negatively by some compulsion, fixation or basic driving force to avoid something unpleasant. This compulsion is seen as one's basic psychological orientation. To discover your number, you have to realize what you seek to avoid, what your compulsion is.

---

each pair write another spell to reverse the first spell. Have them chant their spells.
The above excerpts are taken from the referenced article in *Citizen*. A copy of this article can be obtained by contacting:
LIVING HIS LIFE ABUNDANTLY
702 BAYVIEW AVE., CLEARWATER, FL 34619
813-791-8449

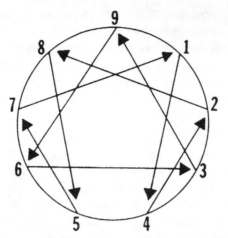

Most Enneagram books have many circular charts, but the "avoidance chart" is usually the most significant; but there are charts to depict time consciousness, or dominant passions. There are even symbolic animal charts—"totems" as they are called. Here, one's compulsion is given pictorial representation: 1's who are perfectionists are like terriers "who snap at people's heels"; 2's who are helpers are like cats "affectionate but with an air of independence"; 8's and 9's do not fare so well—they are like a rhinoceros and an elephant respectively; some take the animal pictorials quite seriously; others never mention them.

The origins of the Enneagram are admitted by all—it comes from the oral tradition of Sufi masters. Sufism is the mysticism of Islam. If you want to check it out in your library, look first under "Occult Sciences."

Consider personality typologies first. Most people can probably have fun with an Enneagram because most of us enjoy getting a little quick glance at ourselves.

Personality typing is not new. Some of the ancients theorized about the four temperaments of mankind; contemporary Myers-Briggs typology posits at least eight (maybe 16) personality types; various systems all have their advocates in some schools of clinical psychology: MMPI (mental health categories); Taylor-Johnson (interpersonal interaction); and Hall-Tonna Inventory (values perspective). The basic premise of the Enneagram is that there are 9 and only

9 personality types; this is simply given as true, it is nowhere demonstrated as proven.

To my knowledge there are no scientific studies to determine whether Enneagram theory can be integrated with other typologies; but that would not really bother some advocates one way or the other. In most cases; much more is claimed than just sorting out psychological understanding. For example, on the cover of the Hurley-Dobson book, *What's My Type?* readers are enticed to "use the Enneagram" in order to: "Identify the secret promise of your personality type; Break out of your self-defeating patterns; and Transform your weaknesses into unimagined strengths" (Harper, 1991). The more you read about it, the more it begins to resemble a college-educated horoscope; and that is not compatible with Catholic doctrine or practice.

Delving into Sufi sources is well beyond this question-answer format, but the more one runs into claims of an "upward spiral of self-transformation," the further we seem to be *away* from Christianity and the more we get involved *in* Neoplatonism and Gnosticism.

As a tool for Spiritual Direction, it seems to me most deficient, even dangerous. The Enneagram is really built on a theology (?)—perhaps ideology—of self-renewal and self-regeneration that is a far cry from (perhaps contradiction of) the Gospel teaching: "Amen, Amen I say to you, unless a grain of wheat falls to the ground and dies, it remains just a grain of wheat; but if it dies, it produces much fruit" (*John* 12:24).

Dorothy Ranaghan, in an extended pamphlet, "A Closer Look At the Enneagram" (South Bend, IN: Greenlawn Press, 1989. 42 pp.), makes these points among others: philosophically and logically the Enneagram remains tied to Sufism; has differing views of holiness and morality; and that the goals of Christian life and prayer life are already rooted in the immensely diverse riches of the Christian heritage. It's somewhat like the transplant problem: medicine is capable of stitching almost any organ from anybody in almost any other body, but the stitching or patch on is not the real problem—immunological rejection is always present and relentless.

Further, on October 15, 1989, the Congregation for the

Doctrine of the Faith issued a Letter to Catholic Bishops, "On Some Aspects of Christian Meditation." As the first footnote of that Letter explains, the "eastern methods" to which it refers are those "inspired by Hinduism and Buddhism, such as Zen, Transcendental Meditation, or Yoga." But, the Letter continues that the document is "intended to serve as a reference point not just for this problem, but also, in a more general way, for the different forms of prayer practiced nowadays in ecclesial organizations, particularly in associations, movements and groups." (Cf. Origins v. 19:30 [12/28/89] p. 497).

The same document "On Christian Meditation" cites a standard taught by Pope John Paul II (11/1/82) that pertains here: "Any method of prayer is valid insofar as it is inspired by Christ and leads to Christ Who is the Way, the Truth and the Life" (*John* 14:6). The Enneagram is not The Way, nor is it The Truth and on those bases not truly compatible with—much less essential to—The Life in Christ.[3]

Gurdjieff and Ichazo—Enneagram Evangelists

According to Father Mitch Pacwa, S.J. the Enneagram was introduced into Western culture through two men: George Gurdjieff and Oscar Ichazo. Pacwa writes: "Both men traveled extensively searching for secret occult knowledge. Later in life, they became gurus of sorts imparting their knowledge to the disciples they attracted."[4]

Reportedly, Gurdjieff learned the Enneagram symbol from sects of Sufis who used it for numerological divination. There was no personality theory to the symbol until Oscar Ichazo developed it in the 1960s. He used both the symbol and the numerology of the Sufis in developing his theory.

Father Pacwa reports that "Ichazo wrote short descriptions of the nine types, employed animal symbols or 'totems' for each type, and correctly placed the personality types on the Enneagram symbol. One of his disciples, Claudio Naranjo, took the next step

---

3. Monsignor William B. Smith, "Questions Answered" (Homiletic and Pastoral Review, March 1993), pp. 68-70.
4. Father Mitch Pacwa, S.J., "The Enneagram: Questions that Need Answers" (New Covenant, February, 1991), pp. 13-14.

of placing the Enneagram into the context of psychological concepts, like Freud's defense mechanisms."[5]

Oscar Ichazo's occult involvement began at an early age. He started to have out-of-body experiences at age six. These led to his disenchantment with the Catholic Church. He eventually studied Oriental martial arts, Zen, psychedelic drugs, shamanism, yoga, hypnotism, and psychology.

To this date, Ichazo's occult involvement continues. Pacwa writes, "Ichazo has received instructions from a higher entity called 'Metatron, the prince of the archangels,' and members of his group contact lower spirits through meditation and mantras. He is now a 'master' in contact with all the previous masters of the esoteric school, including those who have died. The members of his group are helped and guided by an interior master, the Green Qu'Tub, who makes himself known when a student reaches a sufficiently high stage of development."[6]

Pacwa warns, "Knowing these spiritistic and occultic involvements of the man who developed the Enneagram personality system should signal serious concern for Christians, since such involvements are gravely sinful."[7] In his book, *Catholics and the New Age,* Father Pacwa writes, ". . . I believe Christians need to be aware of the Enneagram's occult origins so they can prevent occult traces from infecting their faith in Christ Jesus."[8]

A Word of Warning

Scripture is very clear about occult practices. *Deuteronomy 18:10-13* warns, *"Let there not be found among you anyone who immolates his son or daughter in the fire, nor a fortune-teller, soothsayer, charmer, diviner, or caster of spells, nor one who consults ghosts and spirits or seeks oracles from the dead. Anyone who does such things is an abomination to the Lord . . . ."*

Occult practices put out a call to the powers of darkness and any involvement with them is a sin against the First

---

5. Ibid., p. 15.
6. Ibid., p. 14.
7. Ibid.
8. Father Mitch Pacwa, *Catholics and the New Age* (Ann Arbor, Michigan: Servant Publications, 1992), p. 112.

Commandment. However, through the Sacrament of Reconciliation, we can lay our sins before the Lord and experience His forgiveness. We should come to the Sacrament with true repentance, an open heart ready to receive the mercy of God, and the confidence that God longs to forgive us even more than we long to be forgiven.

Involved Beyond Belief
An Interview with Mrs. R.

Mrs. R's involvement with the occult slowly continued to grow until she experienced deliverance.

Johnnette: Why did you become involved with the occult?

Mrs. R.: It was fascinating and it was exciting. And I became involved with friends who also had the same interest. And we would get together and I would become a medium in seances. It was kind of a fun thing at first, but then it began to fulfill me spiritually.

Johnnette: As you grew older, did this fascination lead you deeper?

Mrs. R.: It led me deeper particularly when I went to university and began to study political philosophy and broadening my values and my ideas. You see, the funny thing about the New Age is you don't learn the doctrine at the beginning. You learn all the theology and the doctrine at the end. It's a process of getting you into it. And then, as you go up the higher echelon of the New Age, you realize that somewhere along the line, Lucifer becomes a brother.

Johnnette: Who was Jesus Christ to you at this time?

Mrs. R.: I felt that He was divine. But I guess I didn't think He was the only one to follow. I felt that any way one could find enlightenment and expand one's intellect and self as your self-destiny, was fair game.

Johnnette: How did you begin to become disillusioned with occultism?

Mrs. R.: My husband had talked me into going to Mass again. So I was attending Mass on Sunday morning and going to my spiritualist service at night. When I attended Mass my heart would ache. It was like a loved one whom you had disappointed. It was like I was on the outside looking in whenever I would go to Mass.

Johnnette: You had an experience in the context of that spiritualist church. What was that experience?

Mrs. R.: I went to this service. This particular night they had a medium from Mexico. And he was a man. And he came right to me. And he asked, "Can I come to you?" And this is their way of speaking when their spirit guide wants to come to you. And I said, "Yes." Just as he was ready to speak he said, "I can't come to you. You have a cross above your head. You have a light! You're sealed! You're sealed! I can't touch you. I can't touch you!"

Johnnette: At that time, how did you regard the spirit guide concept?

Mrs. R.: I considered the spirit guide as someone who was my friend, who really wanted me to succeed, who wanted the best for me, who was sent to me by God to help me. And a lot of New Agers even think they are guardian angels. You see Lucifer is the Father of Lies, and this is how he gets you into it.

Johnnette: Who is Lucifer to the New Age?

Mrs. R.: Not Satan. He's now the Angel of Light.

Johnnette: Did you ever begin to feel that this was controlling you?

Mrs. R.: That didn't happen for a long time. I had gotten involved in astral projection in which you try to will your spirit to leave your body. I would see myself rise from my body and I couldn't connect my spirit with my body. I became very frightened. And I realized there was something in it that wasn't just enlightenment anymore. There was an oppressive spirit over me.

Johnnette: When did you make the decision that you had to go back to Jesus?

Mrs. R.: At that time I was attending scripture classes and I was also dabbling a bit in fortune-telling, card reading, the Ouija board, and I had seen a psychic, and things like that. Scripture hit me right in the eyes where it says, "No fortune-teller will enter the Kingdom of Heaven."

Johnnette: How did you get rid of that oppressive spirit?

Mrs. R.: I finally arranged to go to confession in the priest's office. And I figured this is behind me. I will just join a Life in the Spirit Seminar and everything will be just fine. Well, it wasn't fine because this spirit had followed me right into the Life in the Spirit Seminar and I didn't know it. So the group was praying over me and suddenly I saw the face of Christ as we see it on the Shroud of Turin. And His face came into my head like a laser beam of light and gold. And it came into my head and something came out of my body, out of my voice, out of my mouth. And I shrieked a scream. And I fell to the floor and I took several people with me. It was a deliverance.

Johnnette: Were you surprised that you had been so heavily involved?

Mrs. R.: I was in shock. I was totally mystified by it.

Johnnette: Describe the way that you were then when you were so heavily involved and the way that you are now.

Mrs. R.: I have peace. I'm not saying that nothing goes wrong now. I have circumstances just like everyone has. But now I have that personal relationship with Jesus and He loves me and that's enough, to know that God loves me. And I have found Him. And that's really where my search began—looking for Him—and I've come back and it's beautiful how my search has come full circle.

Questions for Reflection

1. The occult belief system continues to gain acceptance in the United States. What evidence of this have I seen in my own community and locale?
2. When we invest spiritual power in anything or anyone other than God, we are in sin. As I examine my conscience, do I have any recollection of being involved with the occult at any level? If so, ask God for forgiveness and make arrangements to go to the Sacrament of Reconciliation as soon as possible.
3. Many people involved in the New Age and occult practices are truly searching for God. How can I lead them to the truth who is Jesus Christ?
4. Monsignor Smith suggests that the Enneagram is closer to gnosticism than it is to Christianity. In what ways is this true? Consider this question in light of:
    1. who is the savior
    2. the meaning of redemption
    3. how redemption occurs
    4. the foundation of the belief system
5. To what extent should the spiritistic and occult involvements of Gurdjieff and Ichazo influence the way we regard the Enneagram and its use in spiritual direction and psychology?

Scripture Passages for Meditation

Day One:	*Deuteronomy* 18: 10-12
Day Two:	*Leviticus* 19: 26, 31
Day Three:	*Philippians* 3: 10-16
Day Four:	*1 John* 2: 20-23
Day Five:	*James* 5: 16-20
Day Six:	*Psalm* 25: 4-7
Day Seven:	*Psalm* 23

WEEK NINE

"Therefore submit to God; resist the devil and he will take flight. Draw close to God, and He will draw close to you."
—*James* 5: 7-8

Occultism—The Darker Side

Occult activities are expressly forbidden by Scripture. As a result, we can be certain that any information, whether correct or incorrect, that is received through these practices is *not* coming from the Spirit of God or from His angelic hosts. From whom, then, does this information come? In some cases, the information is simply the product of the imagination. In other cases, the seer is a fraud and gives probable information that is ambiguous and can apply to most anyone. However, there are those cases where the seer is consorting with the powers of darkness to gain information.

The New Agers call these powers of darkness by various names such as spirit guides, ascended masters, and avatars. They do not recognize them as evil spirits, but consider them to be highly evolved beings who passed through several incarnations on their way to enlightenment. Now enlightened and no longer needing to be reincarnated, they seek to bring us the knowledge we need on our spiritual journey. Though seemingly infinite in number, counted among the New Age avatars are Jesus, Buddha, Seth, Ramtha, Lazaris, and Mother Mary. Lucifer is also counted among them. He is referred to as the Angel of Light.

Various practices exist for contacting these spirits. All of them involve some form of mediumship and an altered state of consciousness (trance). Following are brief definitions of some of the most common.

Methods of Spiritism

Automatic Writing: Most automatic writers wish to contact the deceased or to receive esoteric wisdom from a spirit guide. The writing is done unconsciously and is not under the control of the writer. It usually is done very rapidly and the penmanship is often large and bold, with little resemblance to the penmanship of the writer.

Channeling: Opening oneself to be used by a spirit or "higher entity" who wishes to communicate spiritual knowledge and wisdom. As the spirit is channeled, the channeler's voice, posture, gestures, and facial expression often change dramatically. Most typically, the spirits are said to come from great antiquity. They are also identified as angels, deities, nature spirits, spirits of the dead, extraterrestrials, and the Higher Self.

Psychic Readings: While psychic readings take many forms including tarot card reading, scrying (gazing into a reflective surface), numerology, and palmistry, during some readings the psychic consorts with a spirit to answer the client's questions.

Psychic Surgery: In psychic surgery, the "surgeon" allegedly operates through the guidance of a spiritual entity or deceased physician. Without the benefit of a sterile environment, using ordinary utensils or no utensils at all, the psychic surgeon is said to penetrate the body of the patient for various surgical needs including the removal of tumors, kidney and gall stones. No anesthesia is needed, no stitches are required, no marks remain, and the patient leaves immediately to resume normal activity.

Seance: During a seance, individuals attempt to contact the dead. The medium goes into a trance and becomes the vehicle through which the dead person speaks. In addition, there are other paranormal occurrences that can take place. Whistling wind, objects moving, and peculiar noises head the list. This word has fallen out of fashion due to negative connotations. Unfortunately, many young children are introduced to this at parties.

Consequences of Involvement

In *Leviticus* 20, verses 6 through 8, we read, *"Should anyone turn to mediums and fortune-tellers and follow their wanton*

ways, I will turn against such a one and cut him off from his peo-
ple. Sanctify yourselves, then, and be holy; for I, the Lord, your
God, am holy. Be careful, therefore, to observe what I, the Lord,
who make you holy, have prescribed." This directive of God is
very clear and straightforward. God's laws are always intended to
protect us from the world, the flesh, and demonic influences.
When we choose to forego this protection by violating God's
laws, we often pay a hefty price.

Many individuals who have participated in occult activities
frequently experience varying degrees of oppression, depression,
or harassment. These influences can take place spiritually, men-
tally, or in natural circumstances and situations. The first step that
should be taken is to go to the Sacrament of Reconciliation,
repent, and firmly resolve to let go of all occult practices.

If the harassment or oppression continues after repenting of the
sin, it may be necessary to seek deliverance. Deliverance prayer
can be administered by anyone who has been given this gift by
God, but generally, it is a good idea to seek out a priest who is
open to this type of prayer. In deliverance prayer, the pray-er,
through the power of the Holy Spirit and in the name of Jesus,
binds all demonic entities from any further activity in the life of
the individual. The pray-er then calls upon the Holy Spirit of God
to fill up with His Holy Presence all areas that have been vacated.

In some extreme and very rare cases, a person may be pos-
sessed by an evil spirit. The spiritual remedy of the Church for
possession is exorcism. Every diocese has a priest who is the
appointed exorcist. Much prayer, fasting, and discernment goes
into the process of determining if exorcism is necessary. This is
an uncommon and unusual occurrence and one that is carefully
deliberated by the Church.

And The Pain Remained . . .

Many people who are in difficult and painful circumstances are attracted to the New Age Movement. Their hope is to find a way to experience the peace that surpasses understanding. The following two interviews testify that only Jesus can bring us true peace and ultimate healing.

An Interview with Claudia Rantucci

Emotional pain caused Claudia to explore the New Age. An avid student, she diligently studied a variety of ideas. All she discovered was a path littered with confusion, and the same pain she had in the beginning.

Johnnette: As you became involved in all of these aspects of the New Age what was it that you were searching for?

Claudia: I was searching for a better self-identity. My self-esteem was low and the reason I went into all of these various areas was to find out more of myself and to find out why I was suffering so much. The suffering was very, very great. And I went into these areas to see if I could understand more, if I could find *the* answer that would solve the problem of this tremendous suffering that I was going through.

Johnnette: And where did you go from there?

Claudia: I was very heavily into theosophy, I was heavily into scientology, and very heavily into those things that are contained in those philosophies. As I went further into that I became more confused, not less.

Johnnette: How did this confusion begin to impact on your day-to-day living?

Claudia: You read astrology charts. You're constantly looking at people's palms to see whether or not their life lines are long. You think you are tuning in to someone which of course, you're not.

Johnnette: In the meantime, what was happening to the pain?

Claudia: The pain remained. It wasn't touching the problem at all. I think the problem was the path. The pathways are enormous. It's astrology, aura reading, clairvoyance, nature spirits, the environment, various aspects of the personality.

Johnnette: You talk about confusion, Claudia. Can you remember how this confusion began to undermine your Christian beliefs?

Claudia: Just from a personal aspect, one of the things I had to deal with after I came to the Lord, was that I had an abortion. When I was in the occult, I believed that my baby was reincarnated. I had to completely redefine in my mind exactly where I was coming from with the Ten Commandments. I think this is an example of where these different philosophies mislead. When I came to the Lord, the distinction was clear. I had commandments to follow, "Thou shalt not kill. Thou shalt not commit adultery. Thou shalt not hold false gods before me." From that moment, my walk with the Lord became much stronger, I received a deliverance from various aspects of the things this confusion led me into—aspects of sinning. And when I received this deliverance, I received freedom in the Lord. The Lord had just freed me and had taken this burden off of my shoulders.

Johnnette: Describe what took place in that deliverance.

Claudia: The Lord just drove out in His Precious Name all of these pathways, one after another. It had this sense of force to it, of this thing going once and for all.

Johnnette: Your quest began because of pain. Where is that pain now?

Claudia: Little by little, I must definitely say it is a process, as my walk with the Lord becomes stronger the pain recedes. It probably is there but I don't emphasize it. It's not the center of my existence. I don't need to buy new books. I don't need a room. I don't need any particular place. I don't need anything fancy. I don't need any beautiful clothes. I don't need possessions. I don't need any of those things. I might need a place to sit—I don't even know if I need that! I can pray to Jesus no matter where I am!

Johnnette: Describe Claudia then, and Claudia now.

Claudia: The way that I was then was confused. And poor because so many of these things cost a lot of money! Peace in the Lord is solid as a rock. This is not an ascended master, this is not one that will be here for two incarnations and leave. This is Jesus from the beginning of time until the end of time!

An Interview with Sue Akin

When Sue began to attend Unity Church, she wanted a quick fix for the painful circumstances in her life. But it was through a deeper understanding of her own Catholic faith and a renewed commitment to Jesus Christ that she found the help she needed.

Johnnette: Sue, I know that when you began to experience the Unity Church it was because of some situations that had taken place in your life. Can you share with us a little bit about what preceded your entry into the Unity Church?

Sue: I was opening up an awareness of an abusive childhood that I had, the mental illness that was part of my family history. And I was going into therapy to try to deal with all the stresses all the painful memories that seemed to be hitting at one time in my life.

Johnnette: Can you share with us a little bit about that pain? What was it like?

Sue: I want to use the word "anguish." Tremendous unhappiness, loneliness, abandonment, and someone had mentioned, "Hey, why don't you come down to Unity."

Johnnette: What was your Unity experience?

Sue: It's a self-centered experience. When I say self-centered, the person becomes the controlling factor. For the person who is trying to get out of a lot of pain and suffering, and looking for a way out, it's very deceptive. It's very deceptive. And you can get caught up in that very easily, thinking that you can control some of this. It's a deceptive experience where you have a fellowship with people who are not Jesus-oriented, not Christ-oriented, not Christian, but giving out that idea.

Johnnette: What was your experience with these techniques, Sue? In that time, what was happening to your pain?

Sue: My pain was increasing. As I was becoming more involved with this, my pain was increasing. And I was losing my faith. I know it's terrible to say, but I would go to Mass on Saturday night, and I would go down to this Unity experience on Sunday.

Johnnette: So here you are, Sue. You have low self-esteem at this point. You still have the pain that you began with. Where did you go from there?

Sue: I started looking at some of the principles that were involved in Unity. And I began to recognize some of the false teaching that was going on in there. The bible teacher also was doing biofeedback. The meditation was not meditating on Jesus or on the Bible, it was not the meditation that I knew to be worthwhile and good. I had to go back to a basic need of mine which was to find Jesus.

Johnnette: Where did you go to find Jesus, Sue?

Sue: At that point I went to a prayer group who was having a Life in the Spirit Seminar. And someone asked me, "Why are you here? What are you looking for?" And all I knew to say was, "I need to find Jesus."

Johnnette: In finding Jesus, Sue, what happened to the pain?

Sue: Pain is very difficult to talk about. It's very difficult to express. It's very difficult to feel even when you are thinking of it in the past. But I did find that once I knew Jesus, I knew Jesus died for me, Jesus had suffered on the cross for me. And He had done it out of love for me. When I came to Him, He accepted me as I was in this terrible, sinful, neglected state, and He has since started to rebuild my life for me. Rebuild my self-esteem. Rebuild me.

Johnnette: I'm sure there is someone [reading] today, Sue, who also is going through pain. What would you say to that person?

Sue: I would ask them to just let Him in in the most insignificant, tiniest, littlest way you can. Just say, "Jesus," just one time. Open that door for Him. Let Him start to work in your life. He'll come in and He'll help you. He'll help you.

Questions for Reflection

1. Many individuals who become involved with occult practices are searching for answers to difficult problems or circumstances. When I am desperate for answers, where do I look for resolutions to my problems?
2. Our society is a society of "quick fixes." From fast food to alka-seltzer, from alka-seltzer to tranquilizers, we look for quick resolutions for our discomfort. Within Christianity there is a long tradition regarding the value of suffering. How is suffering valuable? How can I remember this when I am in the midst of it?
3. Read the Passion of Jesus as related in the Gospel of Mark (*Mark* 14:32-72; 15:1-41). Write down the words that describe His physical suffering. Then, write down the words that describe His emotional and psychological suffering. Identify your own pain and suffering in His. How are they similar? **Consider:** If Jesus took this same pain and suffering that I am experiencing to the Cross with Him, what does this say about my pain and suffering in light of the Resurrection? How does this perspective of the passion, death, and resurrection of Jesus Christ impact on my own suffering and my ability to cope?
4. God calls us to be holy as He is holy. What aspects of my life must be changed in order to respond to this call? How willing am I to change? What are some practical and concrete ways that I can begin to implement change.

Scripture Passages for Meditation

Day One: *James* 4: 7-8
Day Two: *Leviticus* 20: 6-8
Day Three: *Revelation* 21 :5-8
Day Four: *Isaiah* 57: 14-19
Day Five: *Acts* 8: 9-25
Day Six: *1 Timothy* 1: 3-7
Day Seven: *Psalm* 4

WEEK TEN

"Stay sober and alert. Your opponent the devil is prowling like a roaring lion looking for someone to devour. Resist him . . . ."
—*1 Peter* 5: 8-9

Satanism

In his book, *Screwtape Letters,* C. S. Lewis writes, "There are two equal and opposite errors into which our race can fall about the devils. One is to disbelieve in their existence. The other is to believe, and to feel an excessive and unhealthy interest in them. They themselves are equally pleased by both errors, and hail a materialist or a magician with the same delight."[1]

New Agers, secular society, and growing numbers of Christians fall into the first category that Lewis describes. As we look around us today, we cannot deny the presence of evil. The dark deeds of men crowd our daily newspapers, fill our television screens, and overwhelm our sensibilities. And yet, people scoff at the reality of Satan. If he is perceived at all, Satan is seen symbolically, while the depravity of man is blamed wholly on sociological and psychological ills. Personal sin, induced through the temptations of Satan, is not even considered plausible. As C. S. Lewis states, this lack of recognition delights the Evil One. Who easier to fool than one who does not even believe you exist? And so situational ethics and subjectivism rather than God's law and Christian truth shape the public conscience.

Ironically, even as public belief in him diminishes, cults and covens who worship Satan bloom and grow. Generally appealing to young people with low self-esteem, recruiters (young people themselves) on high school and college campuses begin to initiate unsuspecting youngsters into the clandestine rituals of

---

1. C. S. Lewis, *The Screwtape Letters* (New York, New York: MacMillan Publishing Co., 1961), p. 3.

Satanism.[2] Still other young people come into contact with satanic ritual through the overt or hidden messages in the rock music of satanic groups. Many heavy metal band leaders freely admit to participation in satanic rituals, activities, and practices. And many additionally admit to the satanic influence of their music.[3]

Finally, there are those who have come from Satanic homes, often the victims of ritual abuse at the hands of parents, aunts or uncles. Professionals in this field are reporting close to epidemic numbers of such cases.[4]

Does Satan exist? Holy Scripture holds the answer. "Now war arose in heaven, Michael and his angels fighting against the dragon; and the dragon and his angels fought, but they were defeated and there was no longer any place for them in heaven. And the great dragon was thrown down, that ancient serpent, who is called the Devil and Satan, the deceiver of the whole world—he was thrown down to earth, and his angels were thrown down with him" (*Rev.* 12:7-9).

In 1972, Pope Paul VI stated that defense from the evil called the Devil is one of the greatest needs of the Church today; and in 1986 Pope John Paul II said, "the existence of bad angels, including Satan, requires of us a sense of vigilance so we will not give in to their flattery."

---

2. I have interviewed several professionals who work with young people who have been involved in satanic covens. They state that there is a typical pattern of initial involvement. A young person who has been observed as a loner is approached at school by another student (the recruiter). Often the first student is suffering from low self-esteem or is going through a traumatic experience (the death of a parent or sibling, family turmoil, etc.). The recruiter engages him in conversation and immediately relates to his situation. This gains the unsuspecting student's confidence. The recruiter then tells him that he can show him ways to gain control of his life, and begins to introduce him to satanic rituals. He soon tells him that there is a group of people who practice these things but there is a process of initiation involved. He must prove he is worthy by committing misdemeanor crimes (vandalism, knocking over tombstones, stealing, killing or maiming small animals). Ultimately, he is introduced to the coven, the leaders of which are adults. He is then inducted into the coven through morbid and immoral initiation proceedings. Should he decide he wants out, he is blackmailed with the crimes he has committed and threatened with death. According to counselors and sheriff's departments, satanic covens do follow through with their threats.
3. Jacob Aranza, *Backward Masking Unmasked,* (Shreveport, Louisiana: Huntington House, Inc., 1984.)
4. I have interviewed five mental health counselors, one county school administrator, an official from a county sheriff's department and two priests who have attested to this fact.

May our vigilance grow even stronger as we pray:

> *St. Michael the Archangel, defend us in battle.*
> *Be our protection against the wickedness*
>   *and snares of the Devil.*
> *May God rebuke him, we humbly pray.*
> *And do thou, O prince of the heavenly host,*
>   *by the Divine Power,*
> *Thrust into hell, Satan and all the evil spirits*
>   *who roam through the world seeking the*
>   *ruin of souls.*   *Amen*

Practical Instances In Our Midst

This interview compiles insights from Father Paul Desmaris and Camille Regan. Father Desmaris is Diocesan Director of the Cult Awareness Network in Providence, Rhode Island. Camille is a licensed mental health counselor.

An Interview with Father Paul Desmaris

Johnnette: Who is Satan?

Father Desmaris: Satan is the "Father of Lies," the great deceiver.

Johnnette: In much New Age literature we see reference to Lucifer. He is called the Angel of Light. There seems to be this different interpretation of who Lucifer is. Who is Lucifer?

Father Desmaris: Lucifer is Satan. Lucifer is the great deceiver. He hates us and any involvement with him is sure to lead to our total and complete physical, spiritual, emotional, psychological downfall.

Johnnette: What is the danger for those who do not believe in Satan?

Father Desmaris: Their disbelief opens their lives up to be manipulated by Satan. It opens up their lives to all kinds of spiritual harassment and attack. They become the focus of their own lives and they lose a sense of evil in their life, a sense of sin in their life.

Johnnette: In working in your office of occult and cult awareness with the diocese, do you see this loss of a sense of sin as a problem with the people you encounter through your office.

Father Desmaris: Yes. In the Satanic Bible that so many young people purchase and read, Satan represents indulgence and doing what you think is right. Whatever you would like to do is okay.

Johnnette: Why do young people become attracted to Satanism?

Father Desmaris: There's a tremendous sense of powerlessness and hopelessness in their life. They are looking for something that is going to give them power, they're looking for something that is going to give them strength in their life. I know a lot of teenagers, one boy in particular, who used to try and cast magic spells on girls so they would become his girlfriends. In his own life he didn't see his own goodness that God had given him, and so he relied on magic to give him what he needed. Some other teenagers have tried to make contracts with the Devil. One particular girl wanted a boy to take her out to the prom and she made a contract with the Devil. "If this boy asks me out to the prom then I will kill my father." The contract was written in her own blood. And as they get deeper involved they will give more of themselves over to the Devil.

Johnnette: It sounds like you are talking about young people who feel a lack of acceptance by their own peer group. What are some of the characteristics of young people who get involved in Satanism and what happens to them as they get involved?

Father Desmaris: They begin to spend excessive amounts of time alone. In occult magic they are learning how to read, write, talk backwards so that they can perform the spells they need to perform in magic. They begin to withdraw from friends, family, school. Their personality begins to change. A real dark side begins to take over. They lose their sense of humor, they lose their joy, they lose their hope. They become very angry. They become violent at times. Another thing to look for is the way they dress. Especially jewelry. Are they wearing a goat's head as representative of Satan. A Satanic pentagram, an upside-down star, an upside-down cross as a pendant, earrings, or a ring on their finger.

Johnnette: As you work with these young people, is their any hope for them? Can they get out?

Father Desmaris: They can. What I try to do, I ask them what is Satan giving them. Because what Satan is giving them is really their hurt in their life. This particular boy that wanted friends and companionship was lonely. The real issue in his life was loneliness. And when I talked about the loneliness and emptiness he felt, I was able to tell him that their were other wholesome positive ways to find that in his life. That's what we have to get at— the pain that causes them to worship Satan, the pain that causes the hopelessness that brings them to the Devil.

Johnnette: Do you think a young person can be freed from this without a relationship with Jesus Christ in their life?

Father Desmaris: Physically they can walk away from it. I compare it to a Christmas tree. You put up all the decorations and walk away from it but the sap is all over your hands. And it takes a while to get it all off. In a sense, walking away from the occult is the same thing. You walk away from it but you carry that sap, you carry the spirit around with you, you carry that harassment with you long afterwards. So you need that spiritual help of God, the spiritual power of Christ in your life to be completely healed of what you have been involved in.

An Interview with Camille Regan

Johnnette: Young people involved in the occult often are recognizable by what they wear. What do you see?

Camille: What you see is these children all wear black. They wear upside-down crosses. They'll wear the Star of David upside-down. They'll wear silver jewelry to indicate their interest in the occult.

Johnnette: Is there any particular age group at which an interest in the occult seems to be more prevalent than at other times?

Camille: Yes, I'd say the middle school group. That means the kids that are in sixth, seventh, eighth, and ninth grade start to peak an interest in the occult through books, games, comics, some of the material they hand back and forth between friends.

Johnnette: What is the reason why it is particularly appealing to that age group?

Camille: Most of these kids are searching for an identity at that particular age and a lot of these kids who get inducted into the occult are children who don't quite fit with the family. The family might be a high achieving family and this child might not be a high achiever. Or the family's goal might be to be socially prominent and this child doesn't quite make it in the social groups the parents wish he would be in.

Johnnette: What can the parents do when they see their child getting involved in occult activities?

Camille: If the child is openly displaying these things and openly talking about these things among friends, then I would say to sit down with the child and give him factual information. Children are really thirsty for information at this age and can be balanced out if they are given good materials.

Johnnette: What are some of the cases, Camille, that have really pulled at your heartstrings?

Camille: I think the ones that we've had that have pulled at my heartstrings here on an in-patient basis are several children who have come in and been involved in Satanic cults but not of their own doing. Adults in their lives have gotten them into these cults. These children have felt safe here behind locked doors because nobody could get to them. Most kids don't want to be locked up. These children were relieved to be locked up because they knew nobody could harm them here.

Johnnette: What is the message of hope in all of this?

Camille: The message of hope is that people can be healed. With the proper treatment and the proper approach they truly can be healed. They can come to find professionals who know what they are dealing with and who can help them back on their road to health.

Questions for Reflection

1. What is my personal belief regarding the reality of Satan?
2. An attitude of relativism pervades our culture today. How has my own moral code and conscience been affected by this attitude? Does my conduct reflect Christian truth in all areas of my life including recreation, work (school), and home?
3. In what areas am I most frequently tempted?
4. As Christians, we have a responsibility to preserve anything in our culture that is God-honoring. To what extent do I consider this my personal responsibility and what are some specific actions I can take?

Scripture Passages for Meditation

Day One:	*Job* 1: 6-12
Day Two:	*Luke* 10: 17-20
Day Three:	*1 Corinthians* 10: 19-21
Day Four:	*Matthew* 4: 1-11
Day Five:	*Jude*
Day Six:	*1 Peter* 5: 8-11
Day Seven:	*1 John* 4: 4

WEEK ELEVEN

*"Remember your leaders who spoke the word of God to you; con-
sider how their lives ended, and imitate their faith. Jesus Christ is
the same yesterday, today, and forever. Do not be carried away by
all kinds of strange teaching."*
—Hebrews 13: 7-9

Carl Jung's Influence on New Age Thinking

Carl Gustav Jung was a Swiss psychiatrist and psychologist
who graduated from the University of Zurich in 1902. As a boy,
he developed an interest in mythology and the occult. He inherited this interest from his mother and maternal grandmother,
both of whom were known as "ghost seers."[1] When he was
young, he felt that he had two personalities. One of these personalities was a wise old man whom Jung credited with greatly
influencing him throughout his life. In addition, he experienced
much paranormal activity including "precognition, clairvoyance,
psychokinesis, and hauntings."[2] This interest in the occult and
mythology remained an integral part of his life, so much so that
it later formed the basis for his psychological theories. Also
bearing on his theories were his avid interests in gnosticism and
alchemy.

Early in his professional career, Jung was a disciple of
Sigmund Freud. Eventually their relationship ended. The split
occurred over the emphasis that Freud placed on sexuality. Like
Freud, however, Jung believed that the mind operates on both
the conscious level and the unconscious level. On the conscious
level, an individual is aware of his thoughts and motivations.
His conscious mind is "knowable." But the unconscious mind is
a mystery to him. It contains drives and stores experiences of
which he has no conscious knowledge.

---

1. Guiley, *Harper's*, p. 301.
2. Ibid.

Jung's Psychology

For Jung, as for Freud, psychological wholeness lay in under-standing the unconscious mind. He claimed that a person is a myriad of opposites. The unconscious mind attempts to recon-cile these opposite tendencies, thereby, bringing mental health and wholeness. Jung called the process of becoming psycholog-ically whole "individuation." Jung believed that the only way to bring harmony between these tendencies was for the conscious mind to embrace the negative tendencies or the dark side of our person.

According to Jung, dreams are the method of communication between the unconscious mind and the conscious mind. The key to understanding the unconscious and our negative tendencies lay in our dreams. Since the unconscious mind speaks in symbols (intuitive ideas, to Jung), dream work is difficult and demands much time, effort, and introspection.

In addition to the individual unconscious, Jung also believed that there is a collective unconscious shared by every member of every race. He believed that this collective unconscious is instinctively passed on from generation to generation, and con-tains universal thought patterns and images which he called "archetypes." Jung generally believed that the gods of mythol-ogy, Buddha, and Jesus Christ are archetypes rooted in the col-lective unconscious. Within this collective unconscious and its archetypes is a hidden wisdom, capable of guiding all humanity. Through therapy, a person can come in contact with the collec-tive unconscious.

Jung and Christianity

Jung espoused an appreciation for religion and a belief in God. However, he saw religion as mythical, fitting it neatly into his concepts of the collective unconscious and archetypes. His view of God was mainly in the Eastern sense, perceiving Him as monistic and pantheistic. Also, in line with oriental mysti-cism, Jung believed that God, Himself, harbored a dark and negative side and, because of this, wanted man to sin. He had little regard for Jesus Christ and considered Him purely from a mythic perspective, often seeing Him as the psychological symbol for the self.[3]

In addition to Jung's non-Christian view of God and Jesus Christ, Father Mitch Pacwa, S.J., in his book, *Catholics and the New Age*, outlines several other areas where Jung's theories are incompatible with Christianity. First, Jung believed that faith is a sin. He saw the blind acceptance of doctrines as a block between the believer and true wholeness.[4] Faith, according to Jung, is a stumbling block. He favored a personal experience of God over faith in doctrine.[5] If the experience contradicts the doctrine, decide in favor of the experience.

This stands in stark contrast to St. John's admonition to test every spirit (*1 John*: 4). Without the objective standard of Holy Scripture and the teachings of the Church to measure by, one's spiritual life can easily become confused and chaotic. Third, Jung determined that real knowledge of the world comes through archetypes.[6] Such gnostic thinking clearly undermines belief in Sacred Scripture and the authority of the Church. Finally, Jung claims that we must embrace our negative or dark side in order to find psychological wholeness. This is in glaring opposition to authentic Christian spirituality which teaches repentance of sin and virtuous living. Consider *Ephesians* 4:22-24: *" . . . you must lay aside your former way of life and the old self which deteriorates through illusion and desire, and acquire a fresh, spiritual way of thinking. You must put on that new man created in God's image, whose justice and holiness are born of truth."*

Colored by his own subjective experiences and attitudes toward God and religion, Jung's psychology is heavily influenced by gnosticism, monism, pantheism, and occultism. Because more and more people are being introduced to Jungian psychology through parish seminars and retreat houses, caution must be exercised. While there is value in coming to know those areas of our personality that make us think and behave in certain ways, we need to be careful that our Christian view of God is not

---

3. Pacwa, *Catholics and the New Age*, pp. 54-58.
4. Ibid., p. 47.
5. Ibid., p. 48.
6. Ibid., p. 49.

being compromised in the process. Secondly, the analysis of our dreams can be fascinating and intriguing. We must be cautious that self-introspection does not become self-worship. While it is true that God can speak to us through our dreams, an unhealthy preoccupation with our dreams can become a distraction that prevents us from hearing God's voice as He speaks to us through Sacred Scripture and the teachings of the Church. We must remember that Christianity is exoteric (open and available to all) and not esoteric (hidden and meant for an elite few). Finally, because Jung's psychology and belief system are tainted by mythic interpretation and occult experiences, we must be careful that we do not inadvertently become influenced by these same beliefs and practices.

Inside Carl Jung
An Interview with Martin Lynch

Martin Lynch is a mental health counselor and co-author of the book, **Healed for Holiness.** *At the time of this interview, he worked at the counseling center of Franciscan University of Steubenville.*

Johnnette: As we read about the life of Carl Jung, what comes to mind is that he would be very comfortable with the New Age Movement. What would make him so comfortable with it?

Martin: A lot would make him comfortable. He wrote his doctoral dissertation on the psychology and pathology on so-called "occult" phenomenon, that's the title of it. And what he was writing about, actually, was his own lived experience of two and a half years of weekly seances that his cousin Helen was responsible for. She was a full-fledged medium. Carl was fascinated by what was happening there on Sundays. And he wrote a scientific doctoral dissertation fudging his own fascination in mediumship and the occult in the language of split personality, what we might call multiple personality disorder now in the 1990's.

Johnnette: I know in his early life Carl Jung was very influenced by occult ideas. Tell us a little bit about his early years.

Martin: He grew up in Victorian Europe, in Switzerland with his depressed father who was a Christian pastor who didn't quite believe in the divinity of Jesus Christ. His own father's bouts with depression kind of programmed Carl to distrust the God of the Christians. His mother was the daughter of a medium. Her father, Carl's grandfather, used to have his weekly Sunday afternoon seances with his then deceased first wife. This bothered his second living wife to no end but there wasn't much she could do about that. Carl grew up with a mother whose father had taught her the ways of the occult, who herself was fascinated with Eastern mysticism. Instead of reading the fairy tales that other children in Europe were hearing at nighttime she would read him Eastern tales and tales of the Far East from occult sources as his bedtime reading material. He grew up in a house where his mother had been hospitalized for a nervous breakdown. He felt the abandonment, the distrust, the despair that a Christian pastor who doesn't believe in the divinity of Jesus Christ transmitted to his son. And he developed his own interior life where he began communicating with other selves, altered states of his own personality he might say. Eventually through his boyhood as these selves, other personalities, took on their own names, voices, and information, he became connected with sources of occult information which he relied on heavily for his later psychological theories and philosophy.

Johnnette: When he graduated from university, how did his interest in occultism come out in his psychological theories?

Martin: He was fascinated with symbols and he encouraged his patients to dream for him and to get in touch with the collective unconscious which in his framework was the distillation of all human experience that was transmitted perhaps genetically or in some mystical way through all of humanity. And so his therapy was based on deep dream work, soul-work, actually. I'd like to read something from one of Carl Jung's devotees that explains in a so-called Christian way why his psychology is so important. "When theology and belief are highly rational, the direction of the Christian life moves primarily upward, towards the heavens and toward perfection. But when the focus of theology is on dreams and soul-work for those striving into the innermost being of their soul, the soul is quickened at its center. The soul finds paradoxically that the way down is the way up." By descending into the darkness of the unconscious, they find light there. When the focus is on dreams and on soul-work going down instead of looking up to the heavens, the soul is quickened at its center. The way down is the way up. This is what contemporary Jungians, disciples of Jung, are doing with his psychology. And he would be applauding them now.

Johnnette: As you mention this collective unconscious it reminds me of the New Age belief that there is a "christ-consciousness" that pervades the universe. And that we can tap into that and when we tap into that we reach our fullest potential and can actually cause an evolutionary leap in the consciousness of man. And I think this idea is very Jungian. As we listen to what you read we can see that there is a clear distinction and difference between Carl Jung's beliefs and the truths of Christianity. But we're seeing so much Jungian psychology and Jungian techniques in Catholic retreat houses and Catholic parishes throughout the country. How do you respond to that, Marty?

Martin: I respond to that by saying, "Open your eyes my dear brothers and sisters. You are sincere seekers of the truth. You're looking for the source of truth. Why circumambulate your own inner core. Descending downward so that you might find inner truth? Why look to the self as the source of all wisdom when we have Revelation, we have Divine Truth." The divinization of the self is something that Carl Jung does in all his work and what's happening on these retreats and spiritual direction encounters between well-meaning spiritual pastoral counselors and their clients is really very damaging. They look inward instead of looking to the Lord who is definitely Other. The Creator is not the created. And what Carl Jung and his devotees, even those who are adapting Jungian principles into Christian practice, what they're doing is blurring the distinction between the Creator and the created. The created unconscious is divinized and in some way, adored.

Johnnette: When you talk about this emphasis on dream analysis, do we see any other manifestations of Jungian psychology, any other techniques that appear?

Martin: Yes, actually there are. This is somewhat controversial, but when Jung was in the middle stages of his own professional development, he wrote some significant treatises on personality type. And they were actually great contributions to our understanding of temperament. As professional psychologists we value what he discovered. But he began to look at personality type as a reflection of these collective archetypes, as ancient symbolic archetypes. And the Myers-Briggs Type Indicator is a Jungian expression in modern times of the emphasis of archetypes that come from occult sources of information. And many of our Christian brothers and sisters, many of us ourselves, have had the Myers-Briggs Type Indicator administered to us to find out what our type is. And we're looking to discover sources of our own power, our own strengths and our own weakness from an instrument that is based on occult typology. So that's one thing that a lot of these retreat centers and parish weekends use that Jungian influences do tap into.

Questions for Reflection

1. It is good for us to look at the "dark side" of our personality
   and character so that we might surrender more fully to the
   Lordship of Jesus Christ. Rather than attempting to integrate
   our sinful nature into our personhood, however, we should
   conquer these flaws through the practice of virtue.
   a) What areas of my personality need to experience the
      healing love of Jesus Christ and what virtue can I
      practice in its place? For example: selfishness vs
      generosity, bad temper vs self-control, resentment vs
      forgiveness.
   b) On a practical basis, what can I do to begin to
      practice these virtues with greater enthusiasm and
      more consistency?
2. Jung regarded religion as myth. This trend is seen in many
   college level comparative religion courses. How do I view
   God, Jesus Christ, and the sacramental structure of the
   Catholic religion? Many today teach that the Eucharist is a
   symbol of Jesus Christ rather than His True Presence. What
   do I think? Compare my thoughts with passages from
   Scripture that speak of the Eucharist.
3. Many times we need a counselor to help us work through the
   healing process of emotional scars and wounds. What traits
   do I consider to be important in a mental health counselor?

Scripture Passages for Meditation

Day One:	*1 Peter* 2: 1-5
Day Two:	*James* 3: 13-18
Day Three:	*2 Thessalonians* 2
Day Four:	*John* 6: 52-68
Day Five:	*Matthew* 26: 26-30
Day Six:	*1 Corinthians* 11: 23-32
Day Seven:	*1 Corinthians* 2: 12-16

WEEK TWELVE

"Anyone who is so 'progressive' that he does not remain
rooted in the teaching of Christ does not possess God, while
anyone who remains rooted in the teaching possesses both the
Father and the Son."
—2 John 9

The Human Potential Movement or "Create Your Own Reality"

The essential belief of New Age thinking is that man is god. Self is seen as divinity invested with all wisdom and power. Man, therefore, has limitless potential and the ability to create his own reality. His problems do not stem from original or personal sin, but rather from ignorance of his own divinity. New Agers believe that the solution to the world's problems lies within the grasp of each of us. As we each come to see our own godhood, personal and social problems will be resolved. What is needed is a new way of thinking, a new mind, a new consciousness. The human mind must be set free from all previous conceptions and belief systems. We must throw off the old (God is separate from man, dualism) and put on the new (man is god, monism). Man must become *self-actualized, self-realized.* This belief in the limitless potential of the human person has given rise to the Human Potential Movement.

Maslow and the "Third Force"

Perhaps the influence which has most shaped the Human Potential Movement is humanistic psychology, the "third force" in psychology. Largely the brain-child of Abraham H. Maslow and introduced in his books, *Motivation and Personality* (1954) and *The Self* (1956), humanistic psychology stresses the inherent goodness of the self and its capacity for unlimited potential. Maslow saw a "self-actualized" person as one "who was mature, healthy, and filled with a zest for living . . . who has successfully integrated his or her lower, animalistic 'instinctoid' self with his or her higher, god-like self."[1]

This maturity, health, zest, and general well-being is recognized through "peak experiences," sudden realizations of euphoric happiness and the interrelatedness of all things. Through peak experiences one is motivated to seek out these higher desires and finds that the power to do so lies within oneself. According to Maslow, this transcendence is within the potential of ordinary human nature and requires no help from a deity outside of oneself.[2] Douglas Groothuis, in his book *Unmasking the New Age,* states, "Without leaving the naturalistic worldview, Maslow smuggled in ultimate values, purpose, and meaning. He did not deny many of the legitimate findings of psycho-analysis and behaviorism, but sought to move beyond them . . . Though an atheist himself, Maslow invested humanity with the attributes of deity."[3]

Transpersonal Psychology: The "Fourth Force"

Maslow claimed he began to recognize a "fourth force" issuing from humanistic psychology. Transpersonal psychology came on the scene in the late 1960s and grew in influence throughout the 1970s. Today, transpersonal psychology has been so assimilated into popular culture that its skewed thinking barely raises an eyebrow in many circles. While humanistic psychology is primarily concerned with the achievement of human potential and goals, transpersonal psychology emphasizes transcendent experiences which move us beyond the narrowness of self to Self (union with the All is One). As stated in *Harper's Encyclopedia of Mystical and Paranormal Experience,* "Its emphasis, according to Maslow, is on the experiencing individual, and it recognizes the sacredness of all things."[4] These experiences include out-of-body experiences, space and time travel, telepathy, clairvoyance, rebirthing, and self-healing.

---

1. Guiley, *Harper's*, p. 483.
2. Abraham H. Maslow, *The Farther Reaches of Human Nature* (New York: Penguin, 1979), p. 264.
3. Groothius, *Unmasking the New Age*, p. 77.
4. Guiley, *Harper's*, p. 484.

To realize these transforming experiences, transpersonal psychology employs a variety of techniques. These include dreamwork, mind control, Eastern Oriental meditation, and yoga. The desired result is an altered state of consciousness which allows one to achieve a higher state of being (also called unitive consciousness, cosmic awareness, monistic unity). According to psychiatrist Stanislav Grof "the ultimate of all experiences . . . (is) the primordial emptiness and nothingness that is conscious of itself and contains all existence in germinal form."[5] It is at this moment of unitive consciousness that man recognizes, in pantheistic fashion, that he is his own deity.

The Effect of the "Forces"

The effects of humanistic and transpersonal psychology on contemporary culture are substantial. Shouting the pantheistic message that "you are god," business seminars such as est (Erhard Seminar Training), Lifespring, and Forum tear down the Judeo-Christian belief system and replace it with monism. Consciousness-altering techniques such as guided imagery, visualization, and Eastern meditation have made their way into our school systems promoting the notion that all wisdom and knowledge is accessible within. Television and the cinema have produced a host of programs and films which make time travel, out-of-body experiences, communication with the dead and extra-terrestrials seem like ordinary experiences. Specifically aimed at the impressionable minds of young children, Saturday morning cartoons are filled with occult themes and humanistic and transpersonal messages.

Humanistic and transpersonal psychology have been furthered among Catholic educators by the NCEA (National Catholic Education Association). Jean Houston, an ex-Catholic, director of the Foundation for Mind Research and past president for the Association for Humanistic Psychology was asked to address the NCEA conventions in 1982, 1984, and 1989.

Robert Muller, retired Assistant Secretary General of the United Nations, spoke to NCEA conference attendees in 1985.

---

5. Guiley, *Harper's*, p. 485. Quoting Dr. Stanislav Grof, *Beyond the Brain*, 1987.

Muller is founder of the "Robert Muller School of Ageless Wisdom" in Arlington, Texas, where his New Age "World Core Curriculum" is taught.[6] In her critique of the 1985 convention, Helen Hull Hitchcock says that Muller stressed "the urgency of *restructuring* society (and, of course, religion) to conform to a 'global model' which will insure peace and justice and perfect harmony in the New Age toward which humanity is inevitably 'evolving.'"[7] Hitchcock states that Muller's theme was pervasive throughout the entire convention.

Also present at the 1985 NCEA conference was Sister Judith Bisignano, O.P., Ed.D., founder of the Kino Learning Center which she describes as an alternative Catholic elementary school. Her talk, "A Working Model of New Age Learning," was largely based on the workbook she co-authored called *Creating Your Future*. Showing her support for values clarification, her workbook provides a blank page on which students are directed to write their views for and against suicide.[8] Hitchcock reports that "nowhere in the entire workbook was a single sentence or idea which was distinctively *Christian* much less *Catholic*."[9]

Why the Appeal?

What is the appeal of humanistic psychology? For many it is a sense of religion without the obligation of moral absolutes. In his book, *Psychological Seduction: The Failure of Modern Psychology,* William Kirk Kilpatrick states that, "psychology bears a surface resemblance to Christianity . . . echoes of loving your neighbor as yourself, the promise of being made whole, avoidance of judging others."[10] In other words, these psychologies supply the "wrappings"—a sense of fulfillment, self-worth, potential, control—without the "trappings"—a belief in a transcendent God, original and personal sin, the need for a Savior.

Therefore, humanistic and transpersonal psychologies are

6. Steichen, *Ungodly Rage,* pp. 242-246.
7. Helen Hull Hitchcock, "Catholic Education Goes Over the Rainbow: The NCEA and the New Age" (*Fidelity*, August, 1985), p. 26.
8. Ibid., p. 27.
9. Ibid.
10. William Kirk Kilpatrick, *Psychological Seduction: The Failure of Modern Psychology* (Nashville, Tennessee: Thomas Nelson Publishers, 1983), p. 15.

noisy gongs clanging. For all of their promises, they are impotent to save. Instead, they lead the person on a never-ending search for a deity that does not exist—the deity of self. Like the serpent in the Garden of Eden, these psychologies ultimately appeal to the basic flaw in the character of man, human pride— "You can be as gods." St. Augustine summed up the danger of this flaw many centuries ago when he said, " . . . this then is the original evil: man regards himself as his own light, and turns away from that light which would make himself light if he would set his heart on it."[11] That "light" is Jesus Christ, the Light of the world (*John* 3:19). Only through Him do we come out of the darkness and into the light of all truth.

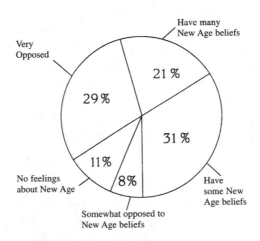

* More women than men expressed positive attitudes toward New Age thinking.
* Opposition to New Age beliefs increased with the age of the respondents.
* Those living in Pacific, Mountain, and Northeastern states are more open to New Age thinking than those living in the South, Midwest and mid-Atlantic states.
* Protestants, Roman Catholics and "other Christians" were among the groups that generally opposed New Age beliefs. Jews, Muslims and those from "other" religions were more open to them.
* Survey results based on the responses of 12,000 Prodigy members.

11. Groothuis, *Unmasking*, p. 90. Quoting from Augustine. *City of God,* 14. 13.

Into The Minds Of Children
An Interview with Margaret Brown

Margaret Brown is a concerned parent and an education researcher. When she saw New Age ideas cropping up in her children's school, she and several other parents took action. Through her leadership a parental task force approached the school board to discuss this issue.

Johnnette: Margaret, you have done a lot of research on the intrusion of the New Age Movement into school curriculum. What was the basis of that research? How did you get started with it?

Margaret: For a number of years I've been acting as a consultant to a number of church congregations on cults and other issues and I began to get more and more requests about that. So I began to study. And as I studied the New Age Movement in general, then I became aware of examples I was seeing in my own children's school curriculum of some of these things in our school. For a number of years they've been across the curriculum in many different courses. For example, the children were told that more important than studying was to visualize themselves as an "A" student and that would guarantee success. But the real thing that started the stir was when the elementary counseling program came in.

Johnnette: How did you decide who would go and talk with the school board?

Margaret: Thirty-five people signed up to serve on this committee. I interviewed them and out of that thirty-five, I tried to get as broad a cross-section of our community as possible.

Johnnette: What points did you present to the school board?

Margaret: We wanted to hit them with three bullets that they could remember and that they could relate to without it having to be something that had to be researched deeply. We wanted them to relate at a parent level if nothing else. Those three were:

> * the illegal practice of religion in the classroom
> * the undermining of parental authority

* techniques that violate the counseling protocol that is used by licensed counselors and psychiatrists.

Johnnette: What would be some of the techniques used for the practice of religion in the classroom?

Margaret: We see a lot of meditation, guided imagery, things that have been intrinsic to pagan religions for a number of years, particularly Hinduism and Transcendental Meditation. The Bible is very clear in *Deuteronomy* 18 about such things as using divination, sorcery, witchcraft, necromancy, contacting the spirits of the dead. And there is actually curricula out there that teach the child to visualize a dead relative or George Washington and then in their visualized fantasy to ask that person for wisdom or advice. And this is part and parcel of what goes on in the occult where people attempt to contact spirit guides.

Johnnette: How does the teacher use relaxation techniques in the classroom?

Margaret: She asks the students to get into a comfortable position and relax. And then she tells them to begin to take deep breaths, or serial relaxation of muscle groups—tightening and then relaxing the muscles from their toes; then picturing a wave from the ocean coming up over their body and with every wave becoming more and more relaxed, and their mind becomes more and more blank and they let go. And then the teacher may begin a story, "Today we're going on a journey in our minds." Or, "Today we're going under the sea, and we'll meet some underwater characters—a friendly dolphin who has vast wisdom who will teach us how to handle our problems."

Johnnette: How are these curricula breaking parental authority?

Margaret: The child is taught that he should learn to depend on himself alone. That he should look into himself for his own standards and values, and what *seems* right for him *is* right for him.

Johnnette: Where are these educational ideas coming from?

Margaret: It goes way back. We see a lot of it coming in with the works of John Dewey. He was an avid secular humanist, he signed the Humanist Manifesto which has all sorts of statements that state that traditional theism or belief in God is the root of the problems we have. And we need to throw this off before man can reach his full potential and solve the problems of society.

Johnnette: How does this begin to impact on the young student's Christian faith?

Margaret: I think it strikes at the very heart of the Gospel message. It teaches the children a view of self that they're all sufficient, that they need no one and it teaches a view of man that he is inherently good and able to solve all of his own problems. I see it as the parable of the sower, where we're trying to sow the seeds of the Gospel. This is like sacks of concrete stirred into the soul of children's hearts to harden them against a view of themselves as needing a Savior. The other thing that happens, too, is that when children are taught psychological techniques to rid themselves of unpleasant feelings, it's a very dangerous thing. Because when the Holy Spirit is working in their heart, dealing with them about conviction of sin and guilt, to use a psychological technique to just turn that off, I think the Bible teaches that this will lead to a hardening of the heart and an eventual eternal destiny apart from Christ.

Questions for Reflection

1. While I do not possess unlimited potential as proclaimed by the Human Potential Movement, I have, nonetheless, been given gifts and talents by God to be used to build up His Kingdom. What talents and gifts do I possess? Have I used them to build up the body of Christ? How can I use these abilities to bring honor and glory to God?

2. The Human Potential Movement promotes an autonomous individual—one who can achieve all things, including fulfillment and happiness, on his own. Consider this in light of the Christian concepts of church, community, and the communion of saints.

3. Consider this statement made by Douglas Groothuis in *Unmasking the New Age:* "Human personality needs to be liberated from sin, not liquidated." In your reflection, consider these aspects:

   a) the effect of sin on personality
   b) the effect of sin on wholeness and health
   c) the effect of sin on our gifts, talents, and natural abilities
   d) the effect of the denial of sin on the human person

4. What is true humility? What is the difference between the virtue of humility and the Human Potential Movement's understanding of man's abilities? What is the difference between true humility and self-deprecation? How is self-deprecation a sin against the virtue of humility?

Scripture Passages for Meditation

Day One:	*Ephesians* 4: 14-15
Day Two:	*Romans* 12: 3-8
Day Three:	*2 John* 7-9
Day Four:	*Ephesians* 4: 17-24
Day Five:	*Psalm* 139
Day Six:	*1 John* 2: 15-17
Day Seven:	*Revelation* 3: 15-19

> *"You will receive power when the Holy Spirit comes down on you; then you are to be my witnesses in Jerusalem, throughout Judea and Samaria, yes, even to the ends of the earth."*
> —*Acts* 1: 8

The Abundant Life

Throughout the course of our study we have seen how the New Age Movement promises an abundant and happy life—a promise it is incapable of fulfilling because it is built upon a faulty premise—that man is his own god. And yet, a happy life is the desire of every human heart—New Age and Christian alike. Is happiness itself a myth or is it attainable?

St. Augustine writes,

> This, then, is the full satisfaction of souls, this is the happy life: to recognize piously and completely the One through Whom you are led into the truth, the nature of the truth you enjoy, and the bond that connects you with the supreme measure.[1]

To answer our question, we would do well to consider the three conditions set forth by St. Augustine for a happy life. First, he tells us *"to recognize piously and completely the One through Whom you are led into the truth . . . ."* Who is it that leads us to all truth? Jesus tells us in St. John's Gospel, chapter 16, verse 13, *"When he comes, however, being the Spirit of truth he will guide you to all truth. He will not speak on his own, but will speak only what he hears and will announce to you the things to come."* Here, Jesus is referring to the Holy Spirit, the Paraclete Whom He will send to His followers (*John* 15:26).

Secondly, St. Augustine tells us that for a happy life, we must

---

1. St. Augustine of Hippo, *The Happy Life,* as quoted in, *The Classics of Western Spirituality: Augustine of Hippo, Selected Writings* (Ramsey, N.J.: Paulist Press, 1984), p. 193.

recognize *"the nature of the truth (we) enjoy."* The nature of this truth is that God loves us unconditionally. And nothing can separate us from it. *"I am certain that neither death nor life, neither angels nor principalities, neither the present nor the future, nor powers, neither height nor depth nor any other creature, will be able to separate us from the love of God . . ."* (*Romans* 8:38). Nothing can stop God, Who is Love, from loving us. However, original and personal sin can prevent us from **receiving** that love. This state renders spiritual death, for we have cut ourselves off through sin from that which nourishes our spirit—relationship with God.

But *". . . God so **loved** the world that he gave his only Son, that whoever believes in him may not die but may have eternal life"* (*John* 3:16). God loves us so much that He sent His Son, Our Lord Jesus Christ, to be crucified in atonement for our sins so that our relationship with Him might be restored. The merits and graces from this eternal sacrifice are forever available. Jesus Christ, then, is the *"bond that connects (us) with the supreme measure."* Jesus is the Way, the Truth, and the Life and no one comes to the Father except through Him (*John* 14:5). He is the ONE who forever makes intercession for us at the right hand of the Father (*Romans* 8:34).

In *John* 10:10, Jesus tells us, *"I have come that they might have life and have it more abundantly."* When we surrender ourselves to His Lordship, He restores our relationship with the Father and sends to us the Holy Spirit Who guides us and leads us into holiness and truth. And it is only through holiness and truth that we attain true happiness and a life filled with the abundant graces of God. God's abundant life, alive within us, brings a contentment and peace that surpasses understanding. *"Restless are our hearts, O God, until they rest in Thee. All abundance which is not from God to me is neediness"* (*St. Augustine*).

In *Revelation* 3:20, Jesus tells us that He stands at the door of hearts knocking. He desires to come in and enter into relationship with us. However, He enters only at our request. He will never trespass our free will. Right this minute He knocks. Let us open our hearts and let Jesus enter now as we pray the following prayer:

Dear Jesus,
  In my journey through life I have pridefully followed
paths that have led me away from You.
  I repent of my sins and I long to come home to You.
  Inspired by Your Holy Spirit, I confess that You are
the only begotten Son of God.
  I ask You to be the Lord of my life.
  Forgive me my sins as I surrender myself to Your
healing love.
  Strengthen me as I seek to place my feet in Your
footsteps.
  You are the Way, the Truth, and the Life.
  Thank You for Your grace which has brought me
home to You today.   *Amen*

Life In Abundance

In these two interviews, Father Emile Lafranz, S.J., and Father Edmund Sylvia, C.S.C., talk about receiving the fullness of the life God intends for each one of us. God wants for us to be filled with the power of His Holy Spirit.

An Interview with Father Emile Lafranz, S.J.

Johnnette: I am excited today because Jesus is promising us His abundant life. How do we get this gift of the Holy Spirit?

Father Lafranz: Johnnette, there's more! And that's the promise of Jesus, "I have come that they might have life and have it more abundantly." We must not be satisfied with less when there is more available. More of God's Presence. More of God's life in our lives. When we were baptized, the Father, Son, and Holy Spirit began to dwell within us and we are meant to grow in an intimate relationship with God over our years. We received the Holy Spirit in Baptism. In a sense, we possess the Holy Spirit. But even more importantly, "Does the Holy Spirit possess me?" That's the difference and that's what it means to be Baptized in the Holy Spirit—where we allow the Holy Spirit to take full control of lives, where we surrender our lives to the Holy Spirit and expect that He will work in us as he worked in Peter and Paul and the apostles of old. And this work of the Holy Spirit is meant for the church today because this is normal Christianity to live out the power of the Holy Spirit.

Johnnette: Father, it is an exciting life when you allow the Holy Spirit to fill you and be the Motivator of your thoughts, your words, your deeds. What is the Church's disposition of this indwelling of the Holy Spirit through the Charismatic Renewal?

Father Lafranz: The Second Vatican Council was called to be the Council of the Holy Spirit. John the XXIII spoke about a new Pentecost. And when we look at his goals in the Council we see that it was to bring the whole Church into a personal awareness of Jesus after repentance, and then an opening to the power of the Holy Spirit that will allow us to go beyond ourselves to be an instrument for blessing for the whole world.

Johnnette: You talk about the Sacrament of Baptism, that this is truly a gift that is given to us at that moment. Sometimes, though, we don't exercise the gifts of the Holy Spirit. How can we begin again, to be empowered by the Holy Spirit?

Father Lafranz: Are you saying, Johnnette, that it doesn't seem to take?

Johnnette: Not exactly, Father. But sometimes we just don't have that full recognition of that gift.

Father Lafranz: That's right. It's the awareness. The openness. The allowing of the Holy Spirit to take full control. The expectancy that this will happen to us. And it comes at a point where we decide to surrender to the Living God, and that God will be our God and we will serve Him, and He alone will we serve. That's the beginning that will enable us to actually experience the workings of the Holy Spirit in our lives. I believe the spiritual life doesn't begin until we are baptized in the Holy Spirit, until there is some awareness of His Presence so that we know that we can be open to the lead of the Holy Spirit so He can give us direction in our lives. Until that happens we're living simply on a natural plane. We're called to live in the dimension of the divine.

Johnnette: And you know, Father, that is what so many seekers in the New Age Movement are looking for. And yet, we have it. Now as we begin to live this new life empowered by the Holy Spirit, what are the gifts that we see beginning to be manifested?

Father Lafranz: Let me make a distinction, Johnnette. I believe there are two sets of gifts. One to enable us to be more intimately related to God. The sanctifying gifts of the Holy Spirit. We read of these in *Isaiah* 11, and we receive these gifts to be more receptive to the lead of the Holy Spirit, that docility toward the Spirit. But there are also empowering gifts that enable us to go beyond ourselves to be an instrument of the Spirit. To bring new life to another, to bring others into contact with Jesus, to bring healing, to bring deliverance, to bring new insight into a situation. These are gifts that we need so much in our Church today, where we're acting with that divine unction, the anointing, where we know we're going beyond ourselves.

Johnnette: You talk about these gifts that are meant to be used as tools of evangelism, to bring others. Often when we think about taking the Word of God out into the streets, we're fearful of that. And yet that's exactly what we see the apostles doing on that first Pentecost. How can we overcome some of these fears, these concerns that we have that hold us back from this full expression in our lives?

Father Lafranz: Only the Spirit can do that and when we surrender to the Spirit we begin to recognize that He is working in us and He begins to heal the hurts that may keep us from being able to go out and share the Lord with others. And He will anoint our words so that what we're saying will have an effect far beyond what would be imagined. I believe that is the dimension of the Holy Spirit. That's what has to happen. We need that unction of the Holy Spirit so that lives are changed as the word is proclaimed. Because I believe that as our hearts are surrendered to the Lord through the power of the Holy Spirit, that will touch the heart of another. That's how our world will be changed—not through new programs—but through the clear unction of the Holy Spirit.

Johnnette: You know, I'm thinking of the fact that when God created us He created us specifically so that we can come into relationship with Him. And all of these gifts of the Holy Spirit, though they are meant for us to take out into the world to help others, they're also meant as a way for us to grow in relationship with the Lord that we might daily recommit ourselves to Him and be reempowered through Him. How have you in your own life witnessed the empowerment of the Holy Spirit, Father?

Father Lafranz: I have to go back to the year 1954. This was before the beginnings of the Charismatic Renewal in the Catholic Church. I was in seminary and was going through a period of questioning the very divinity of Jesus Christ. I had been called to the seminary by a personal experience with God the Father. I went into the chapel of the seminary and put it all before God the Father and acknowledged that I couldn't do it. I had to surrender to Him. At that moment, Jesus came alive. I knew Jesus personally. The power of the Word of God came alive—I could open Scripture and it wasn't a dead letter, but a living Word. Then I began to recognize that I could do things that I couldn't do on my own. I recognized the power of the Spirit working in me whereas before I didn't experience this. But most importantly, at that moment came the gift of contemplative prayer. The awareness of the Presence of God, the joy of being before God, the acknowledgment that He is with us. And knowing this, I know that I know that I know.

Johnnette: Well, Father, as you speak I know those that are [reading] your words this day are being filled with a greater desire to feel this touch of the Lord's presence in their lives. I thank you for giving us your testimony this day and again, stirring up within me that desire to live a life fully empowered by the Spirit of God.

An Interview with Father Edmund Sylvia, C.S.C.

Johnnette: Father Emile shared with us so beautifully about that moment in his own life when he experienced the power of the Holy Spirit. How did that moment happen for you?

Father Sylvia: Johnnette, in my own life it was a process somewhat similar to Father Emile's. It first was coming to know Jesus in a personal way. Coming to know that He really was alive in His Church today. That He was taking care of His sheep. And I felt like a lost sheep at that time and I really did experience Him taking me up in His arms. Soon after that I, too, was ready for that new infilling of the Holy Spirit. God in His own sovereign time and great and abundant love filled my heart in a way I couldn't have imagined.

Johnnette: Coming to know Jesus in our lives is the first step in this love affair with Him. And, as we continue to grow in relationship, spiritually we need to grow with that. Let's talk for a minute about these steps of spiritual growth that are important for us as we come into maturity as Christians.

Father Sylvia: Certainly one of the most important things is coming to know the truth and allowing that truth to deepen with us. What that really does is to provide a foundation upon which God can build the kingdom within us so that we can be so filled with Father, Son, and Holy Spirit that we can invite others through our own witness. Each of us, in some sense, is meant to be on fire like the apostles at Pentecost, even in a greater way, for this foundation of truth has been given to us and built upon over centuries.

Johnnette: And yet we have also seen how Satan chooses to counterfeit that truth, to make it appear other than it is. And God continues to show us through the Church that one right path, that narrow way that leads only to His heart. Jesus is that Way, that Truth, and that Life.

Father Sylvia: You could not put it more succinctly. That is really the truth. What distinguishes Christianity from beginning to end is this personal knowledge, coming into this deep personal relationship with this Son of God Who has taken flesh, been raised up so that our sins may be forgiven so we might take on a new life. Not a retread life. Not the old life redone. But a new life in Him.

Johnnette: How did you begin to see that new life expressing itself after you came to know Jesus as Lord and after being empowered by the Holy Spirit?

Father Sylvia: As Father Emile mentioned, one of the first things was the way in which God's Word came alive. God's Word and the work of studying God's Word and allowing that Word to transform us is a very important work of the Holy Spirit. We've got to be willing and cooperative with that work. Certainly the gift of prayer is a very important aspect of that. As is the call to serve to be messengers of this Good News. To carry on that work of evangelization is something that comes from our hearts not just from one's head.

Johnnette: I'm thinking as you're speaking that the true counterfeit of this New Age Movement is that it is something other than what is revealed to all. It's not revealed to everyone. Jesus wants everyone to come into relationship with Him.

Father Sylvia: Absolutely. And remember what we said very early on—what God really wants us to do is to be alive in the Word that really brings us meaning. The Word is meant to move us from that which is life-less to that which is full of life. And that revelation also comes through the very events of God in our lives, events that we come to know and find greater meaning in as we reflect on God's word.

Questions for Reflection

1. Where am I looking for happiness and fulfillment in my life? To what extent is it satisfying?
2. Many people believe they are so unlovable that even God cannot truly love them. This feeling often comes from a deep emotional wound or a sin that we consider to be unforgivable.
   Sit quietly in Our Lord's presence and reflect on the following. As you reflect, be honest with yourself and with God.
   a) Is there a deep emotional wound which I have never brought before Our Lord for healing?
   b) Is there a sin for which I have asked forgiveness from God, but for which I have not forgiven myself?
   c) Jesus longs to heal our woundedness. But first, we must give Him permission. Through the power of His love, open those wounded and hurting areas of your heart to Him now, and allow His healing Presence to permeate your being. You are His love.
3. Once we humbly ask Jesus to be the Lord of our lives, we begin to see His loving action in amazing ways. For the next week (or longer), keep a journal of the ways in which you see Him moving in your life. Thank Him and praise Him for His love.

Scripture Passages for Meditation

Day One:	*John* 3: 16
Day Two:	*John* 15: 18-26
Day Three:	*Jeremiah* 29: 11-14
Day Four:	*Acts* 2: 1-4
Day Five:	*Romans* 8: 35-38
Day Six:	*Acts* 1: 8
Day Seven:	*Revelation* 3: 20

"Be patient, therefore, my brothers, until the coming of the Lord. See how the farmer awaits the precious yield of the soil. He looks forward to it patiently while the soil receives the winter and the spring rains. You, too, must be patient. Steady your hearts, because the coming of the Lord is at hand."
—*James* 5: 7-8

A Note in Closing

As I have given talks about the New Age Movement throughout the country, one question repeatedly is asked: "How can I help friends and adult family members who are caught up in this belief system?" Perhaps you are asking the same question yourself. My reply never varies.

First, I encourage you to pray for the person who is involved. The importance of this first step cannot be overemphasized. Intercessory prayer prepares the field of the heart to receive the seed of truth. Truth cannot grow in a heart that has not been prepared, and all the words in the world—no matter how inspiring—cannot make it so. Till the soil of your loved one's heart with your steadfast and earnest prayer.

The next step can be a difficult one. Wait. Wait until you know the soil of the heart has been made ready. You will know the time is right when the opportunity to speak comes through your loved one. He or she may ask you a question or come to you for advice. He or she may express dissatisfaction or discontent. This is your cue that the time is right.

Speak. Speak the truth gently and with love. Answer the question with compassion and concern. Avoid a "lecture" tone or a "See, I told you so," tone. Let your friend or loved one lead the conversation; if they pursue, continue; if they are quiet, then you be quiet. With such an exchange, the seed of truth can gently begin to take root in his or her heart.

Finally, water the seed of truth with continued prayer, love and support. Sometimes, you will see rapid changes in your loved one. Sometimes, you will see no change. Do not lose heart. Remember, St. Monica prayed for St. Augustine for forty years. Time is not important, only eternity.

We will be praying for you as you present the Truth in love.

In His Service,

Johnnette S. Benkovic

Bibliography

Aranza, Jacob, *Backward Masking Unmasked,* Shreveport, LA, Huntington House, Inc., 1984.*

Bouyer, Louis, *Introduction to Spirituality,* New York, NY, Desclee Company, 1961.

Broderick, Robert C., *Catholic Encyclopedia,* New York, NY, Thomas Nelson Publishers, 1976.

The Classics of Western Spirituality: Augustine of Hippo, Selected Writings, "The Happy Life," Ramsey, NJ, Paulist Press, 1984.

Chandler, Russell, *Understanding the New Age,* Dallas, TX, Word Publishing, 1988.

DeCelles, Dan, "Centering Prayer Meets the Vatican," Parts One and Two, *New Heaven/New Earth,* March and April, 1990.

DeCelles, Dan, "Centering Prayer and Cassian's *Conferences,*" *New Heaven/New Earth,* February, 1991.

Dubay, S.M., Thomas, *Fire Within,* San Francisco, CA, Ignatius Press, 1989.

Easton, Nina, "Shirley MacLaine's Mysticism for the Masses," *Los Angeles Times Magazine,* September 6, 1987.

Ferguson, Marilyn, *The Aquarian Conspiracy,* Los Angeles, CA, Jeremy P. Tarcher, Inc., 1980.

Fisher, Paul A., *Behind the Lodge Door,* Bowie, MD, Shield Publishing, Inc., 1989.

Flanagan, O.F.M., Father Finbarr, "Centering Prayer: Transcendental Meditation for the Christian Market," *Faith and Renewal,* May/June, 1991.

Flannery, Austin P., Editor, *Documents of Vatican II,* Grand Rapids, MI, William B. Eerdmans Publishing Co., 1980.

Fox, O.P., Matthew, *The Coming of the Cosmic Christ: The Healing of Mother Earth and the Birth of Global Renaissance,* San Francisco, CA, Harper & Row, 1988.

Garrigou-Lagrange, O.P., Father Reginald, *The Three Ages of The Interior Life, Vol. II,* Rockford, IL, TAN Books and Publishers, Inc., 1989.

Groothuis, Douglas R., *Unmasking the New Age,* Downers Grove, IL, Intervarsity Press, 1986.

Guiley, Rosemary Ellen, *Harper's Encyclopedia of Mystical and Paranormal Experience,* New York, NY, HarperCollins Publishers, 1991.

Hardon, S.J., John A., *The Question and Answer Catholic Catechism,* New York, NY, Doubleday, 1981.

The Historical Basis of Modern Theosophy, Wheaton, IL, Theosophical Society.

Hitchcock, Helen Hull, "Catholic Education Goes Over the Rainbow: The NCEA and the New Age," *Fidelity,* August, 1985.

Iozzi, Carol, et al, *The New Age Catalogue,* New York, NY, Doubleday, Island Publishing Co., 1988.

Johnson, William, Editor, *The Cloud of Unknowing,* New York, NY, Doubleday, 1973.

Keating, Thomas, *Open Mind, Open Heart,* Amity, NY, Amity House, 1986.

Kilpatrick, William Kirk, *Psychological Seduction: The Failure of Modern Psychology,* Nashville, TN, Thomas Nelson Publishers, 1983.

Koller, Kerry J., "But Is It Prayer?," *New Heaven/New Earth,* February, 1991.

Lewis, C.S., *The Screwtape Letters,* New York, NY, MacMillan Publishing Co., 1961.*

Mannion, Reverend M. Francis, "The Church and the Voices of Feminism," *America,* October 5, 1991.

Martin, Walter, *The New Cults*, Santa Ana, CA, Vision House, 1981.

Maslow, Abraham H., *The Farther Reaches of Human Nature,* New York, NY, Penguin, 1979.

Mendenhall, Deborah, "Nightmarish Textbooks Await Your Kids," *Citizens,* September 17, 1990.

Pacwa, S.J., Father Mitch, *Catholics and the New Age,* Ann Arbor, MI, Servant Books, 1992.

Pacwa, S.J., Father Mitch, "The Enneagram: Questions that Need Answers," *New Covenant,* February, 1991.

Rath, Ralph, *The New Age: A Christian Critique,* South Bend, IN, Greenlawn Press, 1990.

Smith, Huston, *The Religions of Man,* New York, NY, Harper and Row Perennial Library, 1965.

Smith, Monsignor William B., "Questions Answered," *Homiletic and Pastoral Review,* March, 1993.

Steichen, Donna, *Ungodly Rage: The Hidden Face of Catholic Feminism,* San Francisco, CA, Ignatius Press, 1991.*

World Book Encyclopedia, World Book, Inc., Chicago, IL, 1988.

Other Sources Consulted

Ankerberg, John and John Weldon, *The Facts on The Masonic Lodge,* Eugene, OR, Harvest House, 1989.

The Aquarian Gospel of Jesus the Christ, Marina Del Ray, CA, DeVorss & Co. Publishers, 1987.

Bobgan, Martin and Deidre Bobgan, *Hypnosis and the Christian,* Minneapolis, MN, Bethany House Publishers, 1984.

Bobgan, Martin and Deidre Bobgan, *The Psychological Way/The Spiritual Way, Are Christianity and Psychotherapy Compatible?*, Minneapolis, MN, Bethany Fellowship, Inc., 1979.

England, Randy, *The Unicorn in the Sanctuary: The New Age Movement in the Catholic Church*, Manassas, VA, Trinity Communications, 1990.

Groothuis, Douglas R., *Confronting the New Age, How to Resist a Growing Religious Movement*, Downers Grove, IL, Intervarsity Press, 1988.

Haddon, David and Vail Hamilton, *TM Wants You! A Christian Response to Transcendental Meditation*, Grand Rapids, MI, Baker Book House, 1976.

Harris, Father Charles, *Resist the Devil*, South Bend, IN, Greenlawn Press, 1989.*

Hoyt, Karen, *The New Age Rage*, Old Tappan, NJ, Power Books, 1987.

Koch, Kurt E., *Between Christ and Satan*, Grand Rapids, MI, Kregel Publications, 1972.

Koch, Kurt E., *The Devil's Alphabet*, Grand Rapids, MI, Kregel Publications, 1972.

Koch, Kurt, E., *Occult ABC*, Grand Rapids, MI, Kregel Publications, 1981.

Koch, Kurt E., *Occult Bondage and Deliverance: Advice For Counseling the Sick, the Troubled and the Occultly Oppressed*, Grand Rapids, MI, Kregel Publications, 1970.

Kosicki, C.S.B., Rev. George W., *Spiritual Warfare: Attack Against the Woman*, Milford, OH, Faith Publishing Co., 1990.*

LeBar, Rev. James J., *Cults, Sects, and the New Age*, Huntington, IN, Our Sunday Visitor, Inc., 1989.

Leithart, Peter and George Grant, *A Christian Response to Dungeons and Dragons*, Fort Worth, TX, Dominican Press, 1987.

Lynch, Martin and Sally Lynch, *Healed for Holiness: The Role of Inner Healing in the Christian Life*, Ann Arbor, MI, Servant Books, 1988.*

Martin, Ralph, *A Crisis of Truth,* Ann Arbor, MI, Servant Publications, 1982.*

Martin, Walter, *The Kingdom of the Cults,* Minneapolis, MN, Bethany Fellowship Inc., Publishers, 1976.*

McDonnell, Kilian and George T. Montague, *Fanning the Flame,* Collegeville, MN, The Liturgical Press, 1991.*

Miceli, S.J., Vincent P., *The Antichrist,* West Hanover, MA, The Christopher Publishing House, 1981.

Miller, Eliot, *A Crash Course on the New Age Movement,* Grand Rapids, MI, Baker Book House, 1989.

McDowell, Josh and Don Stewart, *Handbook of Today's Religions,* San Bernadino, CA, Here's Life Publishers Inc., 1983.

McGuire, Paul, *Evangelizing the New Age,* Lancaster, PA, Servant Publications, 1989.

McRoberts, Kerry D., *New Age or Old Lie?,* Peabody, MA, Hendrickson Publishers, 1989.

Persinger, Michael A., Normand J. Carrey and Lynn A. Suess, *TM and Cult Mania,* North Quincey, MA, The Christopher Publishing House, 1980.

Peters, Dan and Steve Peters, *Why Knock Rock?,* Minneapolis, MN, Bethany House Publishers, 1984.

Phillips, Phil, *Turmoil in the Toy Box,* Lancaster, PA, Starburst Publishers, 1986.

Ranaghan, Dorothy, *A Closer Look at the Enneagram,* South Bend, IN, Greenlawn Press, 1989.

Reisser, Paul, Teri Reisser and John Weldon, *The Holistic Healers: Christian Perspective on New Age Health Care,* Downers Grove, IL, Intervarsity Press, 1987.

Reisser, Paul, Teri Reisser and John Weldon, *New Age Medicine: A Christian Perspective on Holistic Health,* Downers Grove, IL, Intervarsity Press, 1980.

Rongstad, L. James, *How to Respond to . . . The Lodge,* St. Louis, MO, Concordia Publishing House, 1977.

Schreck, Alan, *Basics of the Faith,* Ann Arbor, MI, Servant Publications, 1987.

Schwarz, Ted and Duane Empey, *Satanism, Is Your Family Safe?,* Grand Rapids, MI, Zondervan Publishing House, 1988.

Shaw, Jim and Tom McKenney, *The Deadly Deception,* Lafayette, LA, Huntington House, 1988.

Sheed, Frank, *Theology for Beginners,* Ann Arbor, MI, Servant Publications, 1981.

Sire, James W., *Scripture Twisting, 20 Ways the Cults Misread the Bible,* Downers Grove, IL., Intervarsity Press, 1980.

Smith, F. LaGard, *Crystal Lies,* Ann Arbor, MI, Servant Publications, 1989.

Smith, Michelle and Lawrence Pazder, M.D., *Michelle Remembers,* New York, NY, Pocket Books, 1980.

Sparks, Jack, *The Mind Benders, A Look at Current Cults,* New York, NY, Thomas Nelson Publishers, Inc., 1977.

Still, William T., *New World Order: The Ancient Plan of Secret Societies,* Lafayette, LA, Huntington House Publishers, 1990.*

Tucker, Bruce, *Twisting the Truth,* Minneapolis, MN, Bethany House Publishers, 1987.

Vitz, Paul C., *Psychology as Religion: The Cult of Self Worship,* Grand Rapids, MI, William B. Eerdmanns Publishing Co., 1980.

Wendon, John and James Bjornstad, *Playing with Fire (Dungeons and Dragons and Other Fantasy Games),* Chicago, IL, Moody Press, 1984.

Whalen, William J., *Christianity and Freemasonry,* Huntington, IN, Our Sunday Visitor Publishing Division, 1987.

Encyclicals and Letters

Instruction on Christian Freedom and Liberation, Joseph Cardinal Ratzinger, Daughters of St. Paul.

The Lay Members of Christ's Faithful People, John Paul II, Daughters of St. Paul.

Mission of the Redeemer, John Paul II, Daughters of St. Paul.

On the Mercy of God, John Paul II, Daughters of St. Paul.

On the Christian Meaning of Human Suffering, John Paul II, Daughters of St. Paul.

Some Aspects of Christian Meditation, Joseph Cardinal Ratzinger, Daughters of St. Paul.

Author's Note:

For continued study, I recommend that all readers reference the *Catechism of the Catholic Church* which has much to say on these topics and issues.

---

* Indicates a title mentioned in the television series, *The New Age: Satan's Counterfeit* seen on Eternal World TelevisionNetwork (EWTN). The series is available through:

LIVING HIS LIFE ABUNDANTLY®
702 BAYVIEW AVE.
CLEARWATER, FL 34619

PHONE: 813-791-8449
FAX: 813-799-2595

"I have come that they might have life and have it more abundantly." —John 10: 10

LIVING HIS LIFE ABUNDANTLY®, the communications ministry of Our Lady of Divine Providence House of Prayer, Inc., is under the spiritual umbrella of the Marian Servants of Divine Providence, a Catholic lay association with the canonical approval of the Bishop of St. Petersburg.

As Catholic communicators, LIVING HIS LIFE ABUNDANTLY® expressed God's love for His people by clearly and accurately presenting His Truth as revealed through Sacred Scripture, the Roman Catholic Church and her Magisterium. Two Scripture passages illustrate the driving force behind this mission —*2 Timothy* 1:14, *"Guard the deposit of the faith"* and *Hosea* 4:6, *"My people perish for lack of knowledge."*

For a free catalog of programs produced by LIVING HIS LIFE ABUNDANTLY® contact:

Living His Life Abundantly®
702 S. Bayview Ave.
Clearwater, FL 33759
Telephone: 800-558-LHLA (5452)
Fax: 727-799-2595